Praise for
DEAR DREW

"*Dear Drew: Creating a Life Bigger Than Grief* is a profoundly transformative guide for anyone navigating the depths of loss. Melissa Hull's journey from unimaginable pain to purposeful healing is inspiring and empowering. Her heartfelt narrative, combined with practical tools and compassionate insights, offers readers a road map to not just survive grief but to thrive and find joy and purpose in life again. This book is a testament to the enduring power of love and our innate capacity for resilience and growth. Imbibe its beauty and wisdom."

—**Michael Bernard Beckwith,** founder and CEO, Agape International Spiritual Center; author, *Life Visioning and Spiritual Liberation*; host of *Take Back Your Mind* podcast

"As a medium, I understand how fleeting moments of connection with departed loved ones can bring profound comfort. But *Dear Drew: Creating a Life Bigger Than Grief* goes far beyond momentary solace. Melissa Hull has not only lived through the depths of grief but has discovered a path to lasting healing, transformation, and deeper connection with those we've lost. Her intuitive guidance empowers readers to honor the presence of their loved ones in their daily lives, find strength to heal, and rebuild with love and meaning as guiding forces. This book is a deeply transformative gift for anyone seeking not just comfort but the courage and tools to grow and thrive after loss."

—**Laurie Campbell,** internationally renowned psychic medium
·ed on HBO and Netflix

"Grief is hard, but it is also sacred and transformative. Those who have walked its depths and emerged with wisdom become profound blessings to us all—teachers and guides illuminating the path forward. We often believe grief won't touch us, but it will and likely already has. That is why I am grateful for Melissa Hull's *Dear Drew: Creating a Life Bigger Than Grief*. Through her deeply moving and courageous exploration of personal loss, Melissa offers us not an end but a gateway to profound transformation. With raw authenticity and deep wisdom, she reveals the hidden blessings within grief, guiding us toward a spiritual understanding that transcends pain and leads to growth. This book is both a testament to resilience and a compassionate companion for anyone navigating the depths of loss. It reminds us that even in our darkest moments, life continues to expand—and so can we."

—**Rev. Dr. David Alexander,** Spiritual Living Center of Atlanta

"It's been said that grief is love with nowhere to go. I applaud Melissa Hull for crafting such a fantastic book on such an important topic—one that needs much more conversation. I lost my mother over a decade ago, and I can truly say that I wish I had this resource back then. In *Dear Drew: Creating a Life Bigger Than Grief,* Melissa walks you through the processes and stages of the grief in your life and then gives you a simple and clear road map to help you design an amazing life on your own terms. We all need help "moving forward" after the loss of something or someone significant to us, yet we also understand that it's a necessary and unavoidable part of life. As you read this book, don't just read it for head knowledge, but read it for heart, hands, and foot knowledge too. Allow the principles, strategies, stories, and lessons to propel you mentally, emotionally, spiritually, professionally, financially, and interpersonally past what has hurt you so that you can live free, healed, and whole."

—**Dr. Delatorro McNeal II, MS, CSP, CPAE,** hall of fame keynote speaker; *Wall Street Journal* and *USA Today* bestselling author, *Shift into a Higher Gear: Better Your Best and Live Life to the Fullest*

"Melissa Hull's *Dear Drew* is a profound and compassionate companion for anyone navigating the depths of grief. With unflinching honesty and a heart full of wisdom, Melissa offers not just hope but a road map for transformation. She reminds us that while grief can shape us, it does not have to define us. This book is an invitation to heal, to rediscover joy, and to create a life that honors both our loss and our limitless potential. A truly extraordinary guide to the resilience of the human spirit."

—**Elizabeth Hamilton-Guarino,** bestselling author, *The Change Guidebook*; founder, Best Ever You

"*Dear Drew: Creating a Life Bigger Than Grief* is a beacon for those grappling with grief, and Melissa Hull has clearly poured her heart and soul into writing it. Each compelling chapter offers invaluable insights, sharing part of her story, teaching core concepts, and concluding with actionable advice. Anyone navigating the tumultuous waters of grief should read this profoundly moving book as it will undoubtedly help on the healing journey."

—**Dr. Robbie Motter,** founder and CEO, Global Society for Female Entrepreneurs

"Stories have always been a way of passing knowledge from one generation to the next, one person to the next. Melissa's journey is an inspiration and serves as a model for surviving not only the grief of the loss of a loved one but almost any disappointment that occurs when one finds life changed in ways that are painful, unfair, and undeserved. This book is a gift for those who are hurting and have lost hope—a remarkable, deeply personal journey from grief to self-discovery."

—**Larry Drell, MD,** American Board of Psychiatry and Neurology, Anxiety and Depression Therapy Services

"*Dear Drew* is a rare and deeply moving work. Though I've never lost a child, I found myself profoundly connected to Melissa's story. Her beautifully descriptive writing holds painful truths that resonate across time and experience. As someone who has faced trauma and chosen to heal, I ached reading it—wishing I had once held a road map like this. Melissa offers not only wisdom and integrity but a path forward filled with agency, empowerment, and grace. This book is both a masterclass and a ministry—a game plan for overcoming grief with flexibility, reality, and mercy. In every page, she reminds us: We have the power to choose, act, and rise."
—**Tamara Sanborn Pendleton, LMT, CBCP, CRT, BCTN,** founder, Freedom BodyWorks; creator, The Healer's Blueprint

"*Dear Drew* is a heartbreaking yet deeply hopeful testament to a mother's love and the resilience required to survive the unimaginable. With stunning honesty and unwavering vulnerability, Melissa Hull shares the unbearable tragedy of losing her child and the arduous journey of piecing herself back together. Rather than offering clichés or fleeting comfort, she provides a compassionate yet practical framework for navigating the raw, uncharted terrain of grief—its chaos, its silence, its unexpected moments of grace. Through her courage, she reveals how even in the depths of devastation, there is a path to forgiveness, meaning, and, ultimately, joy. This book is not just for those who have known loss; it is for anyone seeking a deeper understanding of self-love, healing, and the profound beauty that can emerge from life's most harrowing moments."
—**Star Rose Bond,** licensed psychotherapist and trauma-informed coach

DEAR
DREW

DEAR DREW

CREATING A LIFE
BIGGER THAN GRIEF

MELISSA HULL

Health Communications, Inc.
Mt. Pleasant, SC

www.hcibooks.com

Library of Congress Cataloging-in-Publication Data
is available through the Library of Congress

©2025 Melissa Hull

ISBN-13: 978-07573-2575-5 (Paperback)
ISBN-10: 07573-2575-0 (Paperback)
ISBN-13: 978-0-7573-2576-2 (ePub)
ISBN-10: 07573-2576-9 (ePub)

All rights reserved. Printed in the United States of America. No part of this publication may be reproduced, stored in a retrieval system, or transmitted in any form or by any means, electronic, mechanical, photocopying, recording, or otherwise, without the written permission of the publisher.

HCI, its logos, and marks are trademarks of Health Communications, Inc.

Publisher: Health Communications, Inc.
  1240 Winnowing Way, Suite 102
  Mt. Pleasant, SC 29466

Cover design by Howard Grossman, howardgrossmancoverdesign.com
Interior design, and formatting by Larissa Hise Henoch

This book is lovingly dedicated to my son, Drew,
whose light continues to guide me toward healing and purpose.

To my incredible children, Devin and Hope—
your love and strength remind me of the enduring power of love.

To those seeking healing, may this work offer
inspiration to find joy and meaning again.

CONTENTS

FOREWORD • xiii

INTRODUCTION • 1

Part 1: Discover Your Agency • 9

Chapter 1: HOPE • 11

Chapter 2: COMFORT • 19

Chapter 3: PREPARATION • 27

Chapter 4: PROGRESS • 37

Chapter 5: ACCEPTANCE • 47

Chapter 6: AGENCY • 53

Part 2: Acquire New Tools • 61

Chapter 7: INNER VOICE • 63

Chapter 8: EXPRESSION • 75

Chapter 9: ENERGY • 81

Chapter 10: NATURE • 93

Chapter 11: CONNECTION • 99

Part 3: Face the Tough Stuff • 107

    Chapter 12: AWARENESS • 109

    Chapter 13: GRACE • 119

    Chapter 14: OWNERSHIP • 127

    Chapter 15: NARRATIVES • 139

    Chapter 16: MEANING • 153

    Chapter 17: EMPATHY • 163

Part 4: Create a Life Bigger Than Grief • 173

    Chapter 18: SERVICE • 175

    Chapter 19: EXPLORATION • 183

    Chapter 20: SPIRITUALITY • 191

    Chapter 21: PURPOSE • 201

    Chapter 22: VISION • 209

    Chapter 23: SELF-TRUST • 219

    Chapter 24: LOVE • 233

CONCLUSION • 239

AFTERWORD • 243

ACKNOWLEDGMENTS • 245

RESOURCES • 249

ABOUT THE AUTHOR • 256

FOREWORD

HEALING IS POSSIBLE! Whether you are aware of it or not, you are coming into contact with this book and meeting this author at this particular intersection in your life because you are vibrationally living in the question *Is it truly possible to heal from the experience of deep loss, seemingly justified guilt, wounds of being wronged and wronging others, and the colossal weight of grief, self-loathing, and shame?*

You have been drawn to these pages at this precise moment not because you are casually thumbing through another self-help book but because you yearn to heal from grief and find joy again.

What is it to yearn? To yearn is to have an intense desire or longing for something, particularly something that feels difficult or seemingly impossible. Sound familiar? It is the involuntary impulse of the soul to reach for relief beyond one's present suffering. Yearning is not merely a sense of desperation or exhaustion in the face of what troubles or haunts us; it is a spiritual response activated within the soul when one is overwhelmed by the voices of pain, blame, guilt, shame, and despair. Your yearning is your innate hunger and thirst for the light—despite the damning facts of your experience. Yearners know at a deep soul level that there is light beyond their present darkness, and they are determined to overcome the known hells of their pain to discover the unknown heavens of their potential peace. That's who I believe you to be. You are a yearner, and if I am completely honest with you, so am I.

In short, yearners are learners. They are the proverbial students who are ready. And fortunately for you, dear gentle reader, Melissa Hull is the proverbial perfect teacher who has, at long last, appeared. What makes her the perfect teacher is that every word in this book has been forged in the crucible of her soul's deepest yearning. This book exists because Melissa healed herself from the immeasurable pain of losing her son Drew to drowning and from the maddening guilt of not being there to save him.

What she has gathered over two decades of trial and error, study and practice, challenge and triumph goes beyond the theories and methods that Harvard scholars like me research in the halls of academia. Her life has been her laboratory, and her discoveries are a phenomenological case study in the psychospiritual approach to transmuting trauma into a journey toward joy.

I have been fortunate to have a front-row seat as Melissa's mentor, spiritual life coach, and friend. I know firsthand how, with the fierceness of a mother, she searched, studied, surrendered, and ultimately survived what remains the most inconceivable loss. She has selflessly distilled her life's lessons and taken them all over the world as a healing ambassador for those struggling to face the hardest things to heal from.

So, dear gentle reader, take heart in knowing that your seeking and your yearning have brought you into the company of one who has been waiting for you with a warm welcome, no judgment, an oxygen mask, and scuba gear—ready to take you on a deep dive into her world of tragedy, trauma, and transformation.

Allow yourself to experience the full spectrum of emotion as you absorb the richness of her stories and teachings. This is not a book for skimmers; this is a book for swimmers—those ready to do the deep work of turning yearning into learning and healing into revealing. And it is not merely a book but a process. You may be triggered by some of what you read, but breathe through it, face it, and then follow where it leads you in your own self-discovery. Pace yourself and allow yourself to have the full benefit of this experience by doing the exercises—be they affirmations, thought experiments, reframing, or deep breathing. As my mentor, the late Dr. Johnnie Colemon, always said, "It works if you work it."

I am confident that you are here now because you are ready to evidence, with your own life, that healing is still possible, answers are still knowable, and hope is unstoppable. Don't take my word for it—read on and find out for yourself.

> **—Kevin Kitrell Ross, BA, MRPL, DD,** inspirational speaker, master life coach, author, and creator, Camp Courage Academy and The Designer Life Coaching System
> KevinRossNow.com

INTRODUCTION

MAY 19, 2000. I startled awake, gasping in panic. After a sleepless night treating my younger son's asthma, I had left the elder with breakfast in front of the television and had inadvertently fallen back asleep. I looked at the clock. Still morning. An eerie quiet filled the house. *Why don't I hear the video playing? Where's Drew?*

I quickly walked down the hallway to the living room. Drew wasn't there. The dogs weren't in the house either. Then I noticed the glass patio door slightly open. I checked that Devin still slept, threw on a sundress and flip-flops, and ran into the backyard.

Drew liked to play in the cornfields next to our house, so I ran through row after row, calling for him, desperate for a glimpse of him among the stalks.

"Drew! Drew!" I yelled over and over into the nothingness.

Suddenly, I saw his little footprints in the dirt headed toward the distant levee and irrigation canal. My heart stopped. The boys knew the canal was dangerous and off-limits, and I constantly reminded them of that rule whenever we went on walks through the cornfields. I began to feel dizzy, disoriented. Breathless, I reached the levee and looked down into the canal. I saw our dogs, one wet and muddy.

Drew's footprints led up to the edge of the canal, where a large clump of dirt had given way and crumbled in.

I collapsed onto the bank. "No. *No. No!* Please, God. *No!*" I begged on my knees.

My wild vocalizations caught the attention of a border patrol agent, who asked if I needed help.

It seemed like every single person in our small, rural town showed up to join the search: border patrol, police, FBI, neighbors, family members.

There was a moment when I stood still beside the canal, sick with grief yet eerily calm. I knew Drew had already gone. I could see his sparkling eyes come to me. *I'm okay,* he said. *I'm going to live in your heart forever, and I'll never leave you.*

Back inside, I gave the police a description of Drew and the clothes he'd been wearing. They had contacted my husband, Joey, who was traveling on business; the drive home would take him a few hours. I sat on the couch with Devin, clutching Drew's pillow.

Sometime in the early afternoon, I could feel the energy in the room shift.

My dad walked in and sat down next to me. "Miss," he said, using his nickname for me. "Miss, they found him. He's gone."

My sobs filled the room. My body shook violently. My worst fear had been confirmed. My precious four-year-old boy had drowned, and I had no idea how to live without him.

• • •

Twenty years later, I stood on a stage in Delhi, wrapping up a keynote presentation about loss, deep pain, and the fight to live through it. I had learned that sharing my experience opened up the space for others to feel their own losses, and after this first big international stage, I was launching a global tour that would take me from Western Europe through the Middle East and back again.

As I walked off the stage, a woman approached me with tears in her eyes. "If you hadn't told your story," she said, "I never would have guessed what happened to you. I'm shocked to see how full your life is." She blinked hard, then asked almost pleadingly, "How did you get through it? I don't know where to start."

I glanced over her shoulder and saw fifteen or more women forming a line behind her. All of them wanted an answer to some variation of that same question: How did I heal?

As I continued on my speaking tour, I gradually realized that I moved through grief differently than most people did. Even in places with some of the richest spiritual traditions, I heard the same sorts of pleas for help. I realized that if I wanted to help others heal, I needed to identify that difference. My mission expanded. I decided I would do more than share my story; I would compile the insights, tools, and resources that had helped me into a tangible guide for grievers.

A few months later, my friend Brian, who had recently lost both his father and his niece, read an article I wrote on navigating grief. He repeated the question: How did I get through Drew's death and reach a place of peace and happiness?

This time I had an answer prepared: "Most people think time heals all wounds, but if you wait to heal from grief, you'll always be waiting. You must actively participate in your healing."

His eyes widened. "Oh," he said, "you mean healing is a *choice*?"

That was the first time I realized that most people didn't know they had a choice about healing—both *whether* to do it and *how* to do it.

How did I do it? How did I heal?

By choosing to take one step at a time.

I started with brute force, willing myself to get through the day; once, I almost failed. I had therapists, group counseling, medication. I read books, I journaled, I painted. I explored alternative therapies and did somatic and energy work. I shared Drew's story, teaching about water safety for kids. As I found purpose in helping others, I became a certified coach. I began speaking more about my experience—beyond water safety and into the deep waters of healing. I wrote my first book, *Lessons from Neverland*, almost as a form of therapy.

So many different pieces came into play to help in my healing, but the biggest piece was understanding I had the *choice* to heal. Once I realized I had the power to choose, I started choosing intentionally. That allowed me to heal, transform, and eventually thrive.

• • •

The art of healing has been practiced in different ways across cultures for millennia—from ancient rituals, natural remedies, and spiritual practices to modern medicine and cutting-edge technology—but the journey to mend body, mind, and soul remains the same. Healing is the transformation of the parts of you that ache. The healing journey is intensely personal, but at its heart sits the human desire to feel whole, healthy, and happy, to live a life full of hope and purpose. I firmly believe the art of healing is not only about treating pain but also about cultivating wellness and balance to fill the space that once held that pain.

Healing is a journey of self-discovery, deep transformation, and limitless growth. If you can understand that my healing journey began with the kind of self-hate you feel when you blame yourself for your son's death, then I hope you can also see that my ability to wake up every day with peace, joy, and purpose in my heart exemplifies the word *miracle*. The healing work I've done has allowed me to become a person I love and respect with my whole heart. I know I am worthy of grace, deserving of forgiveness, and capable of creating a life bigger than grief—a life of love, joy, and purpose. Free from the pain of my past, I'm busy living a beautiful life and building rewarding relationships with my children, family, friends, and community.

Because of my own experience along the healing path, I can wholeheartedly promise you one thing: You can heal too. I believe that statement with such conviction that it drove me to write this book, a collection of the tools and practices that let me release the pain of the past and rebuild something vibrant in its place.

I've structured this book in four parts that progress through the healing process:

- In Part 1, Discover Your Agency, you'll learn how to reframe your relationship with pain and healing, and you'll discover your agency—your ability to choose to heal.
- In Part 2, Acquire New Tools, you'll prepare for hard emotional work by finding tools and practices that align with your personal healing needs.
- In Part 3, Face the Tough Stuff, you'll look at difficult emotional wounds so that you can heal them—and you might be surprised how entangled they are.
- Finally, in Part 4, Create a Life Bigger Than Grief, you'll find the gifts in your pain and see how beautiful life can become when you choose to live from a place of healing and empowerment.

In each chapter, you will read about different points in my healing journey, the lessons I have been taught, and a practice or two that I found useful at that particular point. Additionally, you will find more free resources on my website, melissahull.com.

Let me be clear that I am acting as a witness and a guide, not as a medical professional and not as a prescriber of truth. By sharing the story of my healing journey, I hope to inspire and empower you to take charge of yours.

If you've picked up this book, I know you've had your share of pain. But no matter what kind or amount of trauma you've experienced, I want you to know that you can heal if you choose to believe in the possibility. No matter how dark your world seems now, no matter how deep the pain cuts into your heart and soul, no matter how much shame or blame you carry for the experiences that brought you to these pages, you can heal.

I am asking you to hold onto the faith that you are more than this moment. You are stronger than your pain. You are worthy of more than what your deepest traumas whisper in your ear in the dark. You hold the power to intentionally choose what your darkest moments will mean to your future. You are not anchored to a life of pain or despair. No matter what has happened to you, you are not broken. It is not too late.

But if you want to grow bigger than your pain, then you must choose to search for joy. Choose to believe in your inner voice. Choose to keep moving forward even when you don't know the way. Choose to believe that healing is possible—because it is. More importantly, choose to believe that you are capable of healing. And if you can't believe that at this moment, know that I believe it *for you*.

Let this book help you ask for more from life than the pain of your past. Be brave enough to give voice to the parts of you that ache. Express the pain in ways that set you free. Affirm your positive beliefs and show up as a force of good in this world. Most importantly, forgive yourself and accept yourself; love yourself unconditionally and without measure. Love yourself until you heal. Love yourself until you can do anything. You are enough. You are worthy. And you are capable of choosing your own healing and happiness. *I believe in you.*

All you have to do is start.

PART ONE

Discover Your Agency

IN THE FIRST DAYS AFTER A LOSS, it can feel like you've been tossed to sea amid a violent squall. Waves crash over you minute by minute, and just as you manage a breath of salty air, you're swept under again. The horizon bobs and vanishes, and you lose any sense of direction. Everything familiar is swallowed by the chaos—until you notice a sturdy skiff within arm's reach. If you want any chance of making it out of this storm, you must climb inside and take hold of the helm.

 Exhausted and alone, you may not know where to go next. That's when I want you to look for a lighthouse and point your bow toward its steady glow. Your lighthouse can be a person, therapy, or even this book. I am in the lighthouse. I see you, and I won't leave you alone in those waters. I can help guide you toward shore, but I can't steer. You must command the wheel.

Once you grasp the helm, the storm will ease. The horizon will steady. And for now, that's enough. You don't have to make the journey home today. You don't even have to be okay. Soaked to the bone and weak from the swim, all you need to do is find your guiding light and trust that you are safe for tonight. You will not live your life out at sea; you can find your way home. If this book is in your hands, I know you're searching for your lighthouse.

It's right here.

CHAPTER ONE

HOPE

Dear Drew,
I can still hear the sound of your soft hum
as you tried to sing yourself to sleep at night.
Love, Mom

THE DAY DREW DIED, family and friends surrounded me. My husband, Joey, consoled me, promising we would get through this tragedy together. Neighbors brought casseroles. Clergy from our old church, our new church, and even a couple of churches we had only visited made house calls. Cards and flowers showed up on the doorstep like constant reminders that Drew would not. Amid the flurry of movement, I sat still, answering questions about autopsies and funeral arrangements.

When a crisis hits, people show up—until they decide you are the one to blame. Almost immediately, the narrative surrounding Drew's death changed. Whispers followed me from family gatherings to the grocery store: "How did he get outside?" "What was she thinking?" The police treated me like a suspect, questioning me in the earliest hours of my loss. As Joey's grief ran its course, he began to ask questions too—and those questions *hurt*. I lashed out at him. He lashed back at me.

While I was debilitated by the pain, my life grinding to a halt, Joey threw himself into work. How could he go to the office every day when I struggled to get out of bed to take care of Devin? We grieved in completely divergent ways, and the vast distance between us made us feel even lonelier. Would our marriage make it? I knew how dismal the divorce statistics were after child loss, and our marriage already stood on shaky ground. Within weeks, Joey left me, and his absence felt like a confirmation: Drew's death was my fault. How could I *not* believe the worst in me when everyone who once loved me now echoed my deepest fears?

Completely alone, I had nothing but my deep, deep pain to comfort me. Like a weight in the center of my chest, it crushed me. I couldn't breathe. I couldn't think. I couldn't stand. The pain took on so many different forms—guilt, shame, regret, hate—tangled up like a mess of fishhooks inside my chest. I couldn't reach in. I couldn't pull it out. I had no one to give it to. So I carried it. And every night my mind replayed that morning in a loop, tightening the knot of raw emotion in my chest until I couldn't bear it anymore. I didn't want my younger son, Devin, to watch this unimaginable pain overcome me—and I didn't want to fail him too.

I walked in a waking nightmare. Every day I wondered, *How can I possibly live like this?*

On the night my sadness reached its deepest, I felt oddly at ease. Devin was sleeping at Joey's apartment, and I moved alone in the

CHAPTER 1: HOPE

quiet house. The sun had gone down, blanketing everything in the darkness I dreaded so acutely. I could smell the seasons changing in the air, reminding me that time continued even without my Drew. As I settled in with pain as my only company, I let an idea I'd been considering in the back of my mind take shape in reality. I poured myself a drink, went up to my room, and sat on my bed. On my bedside table stood a bottle of pills. Sobbing into my vodka, I considered ending my life. I didn't feel capable of living in this kind of despair any longer, but more than anything, I was terrified I would unintentionally hurt Devin. The questions, the blame, the outright hate gripped me—a closing argument that unequivocally identified the guilty party.

I thought everyone would be better off without me.

Unable to see a way forward, I grabbed a sheet of paper from my desk and attempted to explain to Devin why I wouldn't be there anymore. I looked for ways to reason with him—and with myself—but I couldn't find the words. Staring at the blank page, grasping at any excuse to let go, I sought to convince myself to swallow those pills.

Wiping tears from my eyes, I noticed a plain white business envelope in the pile of unopened condolence cards that had lain on my nightstand for weeks. There was no return address or street address. The envelope simply read, "To the Mother of Drew Gallemore." I didn't recognize the writing, and something moved me to open it. It came from a complete stranger named Theresa, whose six-year-old daughter had been hit by a car while riding her bike. Theresa talked about the guilt she had felt for running back into the house for a few seconds to grab something she'd forgotten. She said she knew how difficult Drew's death would be for me to carry, how tempted I would be to blame myself, to beat myself up, or worse.

For the first time, someone understood my pain, and for a moment, I felt a little less alone. Between heaving sobs, I read the words that saved my life:

> As unimaginable as it might sound to you now, I want you to know it is possible to find joy and happiness again, but you're going to have to choose it. There will be good days and bad days. You'll make progress and lose ground again. You'll feel like you're losing your mind, but you have to trust that joy is possible again. Every day, find something to smile about. Be careful of what you allow your mind to think about. Fight the temptation to keep returning to those questions—the what-ifs, the should-have-beens. Instead, choose to find meaning. Choose to hold onto the love you shared and never let go. I promise you will smile again. Joy and happiness will be yours if you choose to seek them. If you choose to go forward, even when you feel like it's ripping you apart, you can find peace again. Happiness and healing is a choice.

Joy is possible again. Those words resonated in my chest. There it was, written in plain ink. Someone else had not only survived the guilt of losing their child, but she had also found happiness again. It was the first time I felt a shred of hope that I could survive this sorrow. So I allowed it. For a moment, I imagined that my life might still be worth living, that someday I might even find peace. Clutching that stranger's letter like a lifeline, I came to understand that life consists of a series of moments, and contained within those moments are actions with unintended and sometimes tragic consequences. I could not change the past. I would never get Drew back. But I could choose to live anyway. With Theresa's letter in one hand and my vodka in the other, I made myself a promise: I would stay alive for Devin.

Every day after that, I woke up not knowing how to keep my promise, but I tried like hell to figure it out.

WE MUST FIND HOPE SO WE CAN BELIEVE IN THE POSSIBILITY OF HEALING AND THEN CHOOSE TO HEAL.

It is possible to heal from your deepest pain, no matter how devastating, shameful, or threatening it feels right now. It is possible to rebuild a life of joy, peace, and meaning from the rubble trauma leaves behind. But if no one tells us that, we default to the belief that we are condemned to a life of endless suffering. If an alternate path is never presented, why should we believe there is one? Hope must be demonstrated in a compelling, credible way for us to even imagine healing is possible.

A perfect stranger was the first person to truly witness my pain. Counselors, clergy, friends, and family tried to help me, but their words of assurance felt like empty promises. How could they know I would be okay? Only another parent who had already traversed the same treacherous road could convince me I was capable of walking through the guilt of losing a child on my watch. I needed an example of hope to be that close, that similar, to trust it. The sole proof I had that my pain wouldn't be a life sentence was a handwritten letter. So I clung to Theresa's promise with both arms, like the lone buoy in a storming sea determined to pull me under. Theresa served as my lighthouse. When my heart felt battered and tossed by the storm of grief inside me, I fixed my gaze on her words like a light guiding me home. When I had no idea how to continue, I used her letter as a map. When my thoughts became distorted by guilt, I resisted the torment of my own mind and instead trusted the perspective of a complete stranger—because she *saw* me. And she let me see her too. Hope in its most powerful form is found in the vulnerability and strength of our shared stories.

Once I found that first glimmer of hope, I had to wake up every day and do the work of honoring it. Every single morning, I chose to rise and recommit to my belief in a better future. I looked for seeds of hope everywhere. I actively sought hope out, finding immense amounts in books. And when I struggled to see the light, I didn't stay quiet about it. I talked to people until someone helped me find the particular form of hope I needed to face another day. I lived in that hope until it became something more tangible, until it became actual change. Hope is how I first began to heal, and it is how I believe you can too.

All those years ago, a letter from a stranger taught me that hope wins. Today, I want you to let this book act as *your* letter from a stranger. If you're brokenhearted like I was—teetering on the edge of life and death—I am here to tell you that healing is possible for you. Hold on to my promise that you are capable and deserving of the peace and happiness you seek. Trust me when I say that you can do it and that it will be worth it. Then rise and recommit to that hope every day. Seek it out. Call for it in your darkest moments. Find it in these pages. Return to it when you feel lost or discouraged.

Hope is your life preserver through this healing journey.

CHAPTER 1: HOPE

WHAT HELPED ME: AFFIRMATION PRACTICE

While finding hope was my first step toward staying alive, my mind kept begging me to reconsider my choice. Not knowing how else to hold on, I started reciting hushed prayers I wished would come true: "One day, I will be okay again." "One day, the pain won't hurt as badly." "One day, happiness will be possible again." Eventually, the "one day" fell away, and my conviction grew deeper with each repetition: "I will be okay again." "The pain will lessen." "I will find happiness." With every repetition, I got closer to believing those affirmations, and they became one small form of solace that carried me forward.

To start choosing hope, an affirmation practice may help, especially in the early days. When approached with intention, an affirmation practice can be deeply profound. But affirmations are not about chirpily saying you're happy when you're not. Instead, they ask you to say, "I may not be happy in this moment, but I choose a future in which I will be." Affirmations help shift your perspective in a way that can break old patterns and establish new ones.

I find affirmations work best when I flip my greatest fears on their head. If you are afraid you will never feel joy again, tell yourself: "I will feel joy again one day." If you have never felt like you're enough, tell yourself: "I am enough just the way I am."

What do you hope is possible for your healing journey?

CHAPTER TWO
COMFORT

Dear Drew,
I wrapped myself in your favorite blanket today.
It still smells like you.
Love, Mom

AFTER LOSS, there's a point when the world seems to move on without you. The shock wears off. Friends check in less and less. Neighbors stop bringing casseroles. Everyone returns to their normal lives without noticing that you never will. Nothing about your pain has changed—except now you have to learn how to carry it.

At this point in time, life felt very, very cruel. My oldest boy was gone and my marriage seemingly over. Most of the people who loved Drew blamed me for his accident, and I spent every waking minute trying to drown out the voices in my head that agreed with them. The pain had swallowed me whole. The depression was physically oppressive, stealing strength from my body until my leaden limbs fused to the mattress beneath me. Getting out of bed was an

Olympian task, and functioning only got harder once I was up. I had no idea how to survive the agony of deciding to live.

The daily triggers were the hardest. Just when I thought I had pulled myself together enough to make Devin a healthy lunch, I went to the pantry for a box of pasta and behind it found a can of Chef Boyardee beef raviolis—the last thing Drew ate before he walked out our back door. Bowled over by the pain, I moved to the couch. *Folding some clean clothes shouldn't be too hard.* But as I sat there sorting them, I suddenly gasped for air. Seeing one of Drew's T-shirts was so heartrending that I had physically held my breath to get through folding it—not conscious of the fact until my body was forced to take over. Later, when Devin wanted to play with me, I actively avoided Drew's favorite toys. Eventually, I hid them. If Devin asked for a toy back, I'd get irritated. Of course there was nothing wrong with Devin wanting to play with his toys, but at that point, Thomas the Tank Engine was enough to eviscerate me. I couldn't make sense of it. I shouldn't be the one playing with him. Drew should be.

Within weeks, I realized no one was coming to save me. The people I assumed would be there for me weren't. Some moms acted like I had caught a contagious disease while others angled to hear my story firsthand. The people who did show up for me could lighten the load for a minute or two, but they couldn't take it with them when they left. Futilely, I tried to give my pain away, but no one else could carry it for me, even if they wanted to. I was exhausted—physically, mentally, and emotionally—and desperate for a glimmer of reprieve. Again I turned to Devin to find the will to move forward.

After Drew's passing, each day I shrouded myself in what I came to call my Little Black Cloud, like a uniform for my grief. I pictured it following me around like a shadow. I blamed it for coloring my days in damp, misty grays. I wrapped it around me like a blanket when the only form of comfort I could give myself was the deserved punishment of a life in pain. But if I was going to keep my promise to Devin, I knew I had to stop looking to my Little Black Cloud for comfort and start allowing at least a tiny ray of sunshine to penetrate. Since I didn't know if that was even possible, I treated it like a great experiment. Could I trade a Little Black Cloud Day for a Sunshine Day? It was a silly, almost childlike idea. But I let myself get lost in the hope of it, and almost immediately I noticed that my Devin was still full of sunshine. He woke up every day with his heart of gold, beaming like tragedy had never touched our lives. Instead of automatically thinking *Drew's not here*, I intentionally tried to shift my focus to Devin's smiling face: *I'm happy to see Devin*. I grounded myself in his cheerful innocence and allowed myself to feel good.

It didn't take me long to realize that sharing Devin's innate sense of joy changed the entire trajectory of my day, and I thought maybe I could layer these positive choices like I was rebuilding the foundation of my life, brick by brick. I didn't do it overnight, and it wasn't a perfect process. Much of the time I felt like I acted out of desperation. It was messy, and I felt helpless. Many of the steps I took in the early days were as mundane as brushing my teeth regularly again. They felt more like survival than healing. But during this time, I realized my choices were either *healing* or *hurting*. I could see kindness in the smallest acts of self-care, and that was all the healing I needed to do that day. I moved from one comforting choice to the next, and I let that be enough.

As I felt ready, I pushed myself to focus on my physical health. I realized that the *physical* sluggishness that came with depression kept me stuck in my *emotional* pain. The heaviness in my body triggered the heaviness in my heart. I could lie on the couch fighting off my thoughts for only so long. Eventually, I began to crave distraction, so I tried to choose healthy forms: I prioritized sleep. I committed to moving my body. I mustered every ounce of energy I had to feed myself healthy meals with real, fresh foods. If I could get through the basics of caring for my physical body, I would avoid making the depression worse, and that felt like massive progress.

In addition to layering positive choices, I limited the painful reminders in my immediate surroundings. I removed our *Thomas the Tank Engine* DVD from the house, along with some of Drew's other favorite movies, CDs, and toys. I knew certain genres of film or music would trigger me, and I made sure I was never in a position where I had to bear them. I couldn't visit certain places on our property, like the bricks in Drew's playroom that he had marked with white paint handprints. These triggers were worse than emotional quicksand—they were emotional hot lava, and I knew they would engulf me. So I spared myself.

In my darkest moments, I turned to affirmations, though I didn't yet believe them. "One day I will be okay again," I repeated over and over. "My pain is a reflection of the love I shared with Drew," I reminded myself when I wanted to succumb to heartbreak. "I never meant to hurt my son," I said when the guilt threatened to consume me. The simple act of trying to believe somehow made a difference in the moments when I questioned everything, including my resolve to live.

Though I found relief in small ways every day, I enlisted help as well. I saw religious advisors, counselors, and therapists. I learned about the stages of grief, and I did my best to talk through the trauma.

It helped, but when I spoke to a therapist or counselor, I questioned whether they could understand, and I struggled to explain that losing a child felt unsurvivable. I needed to witness other parents who had come through this pain if I wanted to believe I could too. So I tried support groups, which did help me feel less alone, but they also kept me stuck in the pain; hearing the heartbreak of another person's loss triggered my own. Only when another parent spoke of moving *through* the grief and into happiness again did I obtain some relief from my suffering.

It was enough to help me choose another day.

WE MUST FIND WAYS TO GIVE OURSELVES COMFORT TO REGAIN THE POSSIBILITY OF MOVING FORWARD.

Nothing in this phase of my grief was accidental. There was no relief without the dedicated decision to give myself the time and grace to feel it. With each small act of self-care, I was rebuilding an environment where I felt safe to reel or heal—whatever I needed in that moment. While it felt like pure survival at the time, now I can see that I was also laying a sturdy foundation for healing; the work is not easy, and I had to stop the bleeding before the wound could begin to mend.

The emotional pain of grief or trauma takes a physical and mental toll. Pushing through it is like running a marathon while you have the flu. You should be in bed resting and drinking fluids, but instead you're pounding the pavement until your body collapses from the effort. You can still run a marathon, but first you must regain your strength while you recover from the initial loss. Moments of comfort and relief are essential because they build your strength for what comes next.

These moments of comfort will look different for everyone, and they will likely change over time, possibly from minute to minute. Rest might work for a time, but your mind may crave distraction as your physical health returns. Some people will find support in the arms of loved ones and the witnessing of group therapy. Others may not have the luxury of a support system. One griever might clean out their loved one's room right away; another might keep the room untouched for years. You are the one who deserves comfort, so choose the steps and acts of self-care that make *you* feel better—not anyone else.

You may want to carve out the space and time to ask yourself what you need. Perhaps lean on the support of your village so you can spend time caring for yourself. Maybe you take a trip or a leave of absence. But when you ask the question, you must listen to the answer and then dedicate time for it. No one else is going to do it for you.

Finally, I want to remind you that you deserve comfort and relief in whatever form you need—as long as you stay within the limits of safe and healthy choices. You do not need to earn this right. You don't need to prove you're worthy of healing—to yourself or anyone else. Needing comfort is not a weakness, a failing, or something to apologize for; it is a natural, necessary, and healthy part of the healing process. Even when we can't see the light at the end of the tunnel quite yet, these moments of respite create the opportunity to see it when we are ready. Until then, hug your pillow, walk aimlessly through the park, call everyone over, and then send them home. Take comfort wherever you can.

WHAT HELPED ME: FIFTEEN-MINUTE TIMER

While I limited the triggers in my environment, they still lived in my head. Pervasive thoughts of guilt and blame were my own personal poison that I could drink whenever my self-sabotage became stronger than my will to quiet it. I wanted to not think about Drew's death—for a moment at least. So I did the only thing I could think of to escape the pain: I set a timer for fifteen minutes, and I actively tried to not think about his passing until that bell dinged. Happy memories and good times were fair game. I could remember Drew's life, but I would not allow my thoughts to go down the road of negativity to his death. If work or chores or my daily to-do list popped into my head, that was fine. I could think about anything except the pain. If I started to falter, I would pause, say *no* loudly in my head, and return to the positive thought I had chosen for that day's session. I struggled at first, but with practice, I found relief in those fifteen minutes, and afterward I felt lighter. Once I realized I could take my mind off the pain, if only for seconds at a time, going about my day felt the tiniest bit easier.

Setting a timer can help you feel—or not feel—whatever you need most. If you are overwhelmed with negative emotions, focus on positive emotions for that short time. If you feel alone or isolated, connect to a sense of support from within, or simply feel the support of the ground beneath you. At first, you may not find any relief within those fifteen minutes, but with time and practice, this tool can help you return to a basic level of functioning. In the beginning, count your progress in minutes. Start with whatever you can handle—sixty seconds can be a massive accomplishment. Build from there. Eventually your fifteen minutes will turn into thirty minutes and so on, until one day you'll stop and realize you survived a whole day without tears.

CHAPTER THREE
PREPARATION

Dear Drew,
The smell of freshly baked snickerdoodles
always brings back memories of the way you'd
peek over the counter, waiting for them to cool
so you could eat the first one.
Love, Mom

LOSING DREW CHANGED EVERYTHING. I felt so profoundly different that stepping outside my front door seemed like entering uncharted territory. After withdrawing so deeply into my cave of grief, the world did not look the same when I summoned the courage to peer outside. Inside protective walls, certain things felt doable: getting dressed, cooking a meal, vacuuming the house. I had that part figured out, mostly. But outside, my footing was precarious. I needed time to process the radical change that had upended my entire life. Gradually, as the fog of loss began to lift, after weeks or months (it was all a blur), I knew I had to reengage with the outside world again.

At first, I was very methodical. Certain activities were safe, such as picking up a takeout order for dinner, but others I avoided, such as having coffee with other school moms. Some places were treacherous but unavoidable, like the grocery store. One good day, I felt brave enough to stop at Target, only to see one of Drew's classmates shopping with his mom. As they turned into my aisle, I watched the panic on her face as she recognized me. *She has no idea what to say.* We both stared at the empty seat in my shopping cart. "How's Devin doing?" she asked timidly. At this point, every word landed like judgment, even when it was simply concern, so what I heard was "How is Devin handling the pain you brought into his life?" Clouded by grief, everything became a trigger. After a moment of awkwardness, I did my best to smile and make small talk, and as soon as she was out of eyeshot, I ran out of Target, tears streaming down my face.

Surprise triggers were the worst, but the anticipated ones came with their own brand of struggle. What do you do when you're invited to a baby shower within months of losing your child? Inevitably, Devin received an invitation to a classmate's birthday party, and I knew it would be difficult for me. I could not wing it. A few days before the party, I called the birthday girl's mom. "We're definitely going to be there, but I wanted to get ahead of a potentially tricky situation. I might struggle a little bit, but if I do, I'll step outside and take a minute. It's all right to give me space. In fact, it helps. I promise if I need support, I'll ask for it. Otherwise, I'd love to make this day about your daughter and not draw the focus to me." On the day of the party, I felt a little less anxiety because I had communicated my plan.

School drop-off and pickup were always emotionally fraught territory. Aside from the expected triggers—the tree Drew planted, siblings leaving school together—surprise ones popped up too. One afternoon, when I picked up Devin, one of Drew's friends ran up to me, sharing with pride that she had talked to Drew at his gravesite. Her mom handed me a photo she had taken of Drew, one I had never seen. Blindsided by the rush of emotions, I instantly began sobbing in the middle of the parking lot. I hated being such a spectacle, but my feelings didn't give me much choice. Well-intended people tended to linger around me, investigating my expressions and dashing to my side as though I were constantly on the verge of disaster—which I often was, but the attention only made things worse.

When I lost emotional control in front of groups of people, I felt intense pressure to put myself back together for Devin's sake as well as my own. Children are innocent; they have no filters. If they saw me crying, they would ask Devin, "Is your mom crying because your brother died?" Then Devin would come ask, "Mama, are you okay? Are you sad because of Drew?" It was hard enough navigating these conversations in the comfort of our home—I didn't want to share my grief with an audience. It didn't feel safe to fall apart in public. I needed to be in a private place of emotional safety to maintain my balance.

More surprising than the unexpected triggers were the moments that should have triggered me but didn't. Drew loved the red Power Ranger; he *had* to be the red one when he played Power Rangers with Devin. When Drew loved something, he carried it everywhere, so for a long time, his Happy Meal–sized figurine went everywhere Drew did. He put it in his backpack. He took it to dinner. Part of me wondered if he had taken it with him on the morning of his accident. So when I found that red Power Ranger tucked behind some toys in his bedroom, it felt like Drew had sent me a gift. Following an instinct, I started carrying it everywhere too. That Power Ranger lived in my purse for a good year, and for many years after that, it stood in coveted positions around our house. (I have since given it to Devin, so *he* can be the red Power Ranger now.)

I remember thinking how odd it was that the red Power Ranger made me feel better rather than worse. Then one Saturday morning, at a soccer game, Devin accidentally scored a goal against his own team—the same way Drew always did. I smiled at the thought of Drew out there on the soccer field beside Devin, mischievously guiding him toward the wrong goal. When I let out a laugh, I swore I heard Drew's raspy chuckle too. I never could predict how grief would hit me—with laughter or tears.

One moment I would feel passable and like I was making progress; an hour later, I would be sobbing in public without a breath of notice, desperately trying to control my thoughts. *I thought I was doing better than this. Why am I all the way back here again?* I would spend hours preparing and caring for myself so I could walk out the door confident I would finally have a good day. Then—*boom*—a trigger would knock me off my feet. I hated that. I hated giving up all my progress to a trigger I never saw coming. *How does this keep happening? How can I stop it from happening so intensely and so quickly?* I needed to figure out a way to honor my grief while staying in an emotionally healthy headspace—because something tougher than a birthday party was coming my way.

Before Drew's accident in May, I had signed up the boys for summer swimming lessons. In preparation, I had bought matching swim bags, goggles, and monogrammed towels. But when it came time for the first lesson, I needed only one bag. Because three-year-old Devin did not truly understand what had happened to

CHAPTER 3: PREPARATION

Drew, he was excited for his swimming lessons. I knew—now more than ever—how important the lessons were for his safety, but I struggled with the prospect. When kids learn to swim, they don't yet know how to breathe or move in the water, and their initial attempts can look a lot like drowning. When I watched Devin learn to swim, it was impossible for me not to imagine what it was like for Drew to drown. I didn't know how to control the images my mind created of his final moments. As Devin became more and more excited before each lesson, I became increasingly anxious. I wanted to be present for Devin, to share in his excitement, so I had to figure out a way to redirect my thoughts while he was in the water.

Twice a week, as Devin got ready for his swimming lesson, I got myself ready too. I started by acknowledging the tough emotions. *This will be hard. It's all right if I can't watch Devin swim. The other moms will understand if I need to walk away.* That helped, but I still needed to stop disturbing mental images from destabilizing me. I decided to choose a specific, happy memory of Drew before each lesson: Drew painting in his highchair, Drew freezing like a statue for pictures, Drew running around in nothing but a cowboy hat. Then, when I inevitably thought of his drowning, I willed my mind toward that preidentified happy memory. *It's okay if I think of Drew, but I'm going to think of him flying down the slide at McDonald's PlayPlace, his hair lifting off his face.* The more detail I could remember, the better this technique worked.

Fortunately, Devin's swimming lessons took place at a friend's home, and everyone showed me compassion. Surrounded by people I trusted, I could safely fall apart—and at times, I did. But I still didn't want to disintegrate in front of everyone, so I decided to communicate exactly what I needed to my friends: "I'll probably need to take some time to myself today. It's not personal. You've shown me such compassion and support. You're not doing anything wrong. I simply need to protect my mental state, and that takes a lot of focused breathing and concentration. You don't need to ask if I'm all right. I'll come to you if I need you."

Essentially, I was telling people to give me space while simultaneously asking them to stay close in case I needed them. I understood how confusing or unfair that could seem, and these requests felt awkward and clunky at first. But they were necessary, and the people who loved me understood. They welcomed my open communication because then they better knew how to help me.

With these practices in place—preparing for known triggers, preparing for unexpected triggers, preparing to communicate with people—my agitation and anxiety lessened. Sometimes I clutched that little red Power Ranger like it was Drew's fighting spirit and basked in the sunshine as I took another deep breath. Eventually, I sat with the other moms for longer periods, staying present and waving to Devin whenever he looked to me for encouragement.

WE CAN LEARN TO PREPARE FOR AND NAVIGATE OUR TRIGGERS IN WAYS THAT CREATE SMALL PROGRESS INSTEAD OF DEEPER PAIN.

The unpredictability of healing from loss can be disorienting at best and completely destabilizing at worst. You feel like you should be able to get through basic tasks and events, but after loss, the most insignificant detail can send you straight down the abyss. You never know when grief will sneak up on you, and even when it is expected, the anticipation brings its own challenges. But we don't have to live at the whim of our grief; doing so can sometimes deepen our trauma and slow our recovery. During the early stages of grief, there is nothing more important than encouraging and protecting a healthy mental state, especially in the toughest moments. This is the time to be gentle with yourself. At first, you might need self-assessment—little check-ins—on an almost minute-to-minute basis. Over time, those consistent, intentional check-ins build into an awareness, and later a resilience, that provides the strength to face grief's unpredictability.

Once we do feel ready to reengage with the world again—when we're ready to step outside our cave of grief—preparation helps. Over time, I learned to build up my inner resources and prepare my mental state before going into tough or unpredictable situations, a process I called "preloading." In my mind, I was loading the programming I needed to tackle the specific challenge ahead, and it quickly became a tool I reached for daily. I would pull up my calendar, look at my schedule, and identify the tricky points. Then I would plan my day around those events, allowing myself time beforehand to prepare my mind and body as well as to communicate my needs to others. Even if things didn't always work the way I hoped, this practice made the unpredictable nature of my emotions feel slightly less threatening. For a whole host of reasons, preloading became a vital part of navigating my day in a way that built me up instead of tearing me down.

Your preloading, however, will look different from mine. Preloading is based on a set of practices and tools that help us move beyond default reactions and produce more positive results in our toughest moments. Initially, we must spend time discovering those practices. Breathwork and affirmations, for example, helped me get grounded before I left the house for school pickup. Pictures and preidentified happy memories helped during Devin's swim lessons, and those clumsy but honest conversations about my needs always helped soothe my anxiety. While we will continue to cover more healing tools throughout this book, I encourage you to explore the preloading practices that work for you: journaling, meditation, visualizations, music, support groups, exercise, creative expression, and more. Preloading is about learning to care for your body and mind in ways that honor your immediate needs. It also requires some planning ahead. With practice, you can learn to navigate your triggers in a way that builds up your inner strength instead of dismantling it. You can go into difficult, unpredictable situations with a resilient mindset. That mindset might not always stick; pervasive negative thoughts will creep back in (we are human, after all), but preloading can help during a time when few things do.

In addition to preloading, one of the best things I could do to support myself was not let other people guess what I needed. People meant well, but often, through no fault of their own, they guessed wrong. I treasure the pictures, cards, and gifts my friends and family gave me. They were acts of kindness and courage, but without understanding exactly what I needed, sometimes we both left a well-intentioned interaction feeling awful. I quickly learned it helped all parties if I communicated proactively, even if what I said came out awkwardly. Gradually, I began saying things like "I appreciate this [photo, drawing, gift]. It means so much to me. Thank you. Next time, do you think you could give me a heads-up? It's hard for me to take this in right now and still be present for Devin." I would simply be honest, without sharing too much. I didn't need to let people into the intimate details of my healing process, but explaining the basics of what helped and what didn't allowed everyone to feel more at ease.

I went so far as to write out and practice a few short statements, so I wouldn't need to come up with anything on the spot while also trying to manage a trigger:

- "I appreciate your care and concern. I'm not in a place where I can talk about this right now. Do you mind if I just thank you, and we can talk more another time?"
- "Sometimes I need to take space to feel what I need to feel. I'll come back, but please give me that space and privacy in the meantime. If I need help, I promise I'll come to you."
- "I could use your help today. I want to keep the focus on what's important, instead of drawing it to myself. If you see me struggle, could you try not to draw attention to it? I'll let you know if I'm not all right, but I need you to trust that I know my limitations. I don't need anyone to fall apart for me—I've got that covered."

You are welcome to use any of these statements or adapt them into your own words. You get to set the boundaries around your grief. You are also responsible for opening up those boundaries when you feel ready. While that might be confusing to people at first, the ones who matter will accept it. With their help and intentional preparation, you will learn how to navigate your triggers. The process might be slow and clunky, but over time, you'll stop losing so much ground before you recognize what is happening. And that truly makes a difference.

WHAT HELPED ME: TRIGGER JOURNAL

To identify and navigate our triggers, we must be aware of what triggers us, what brings us back to a place of safety, and what makes the downward spiral worse. That's not an easy task for anyone, especially someone who is in the throes of grief. To help with this process, I started making a list of places, activities, and people that made me feel supported: spending time in Drew's treehouse with Devin, watching hummingbirds drink from the birdfeeders, standing among the sunflowers in the garden, writing in my journal. I also made a list of destabilizing factors: Drew's old preschool, Target, Drew's favorite restaurant. Over time, the lists evolved, and eventually I didn't need them anymore. But in the meantime, it helped to see my triggers and tools written out in plain ink.

If you're struggling to identify your triggers, start by writing down a few obvious ones. Then leave it be. As you encounter tricky situations or highly emotional days, jot down the words, places, feelings, and expressions that led to your tipping point. You don't have to solve anything immediately. As you practice preloading, track the tools and practices you use, and make note of what worked and what didn't. This tracking needn't be complex or heavy—make it a simple exploration into cause and effect. Focus on the results—not your perceived failure or success—to guide you forward.

CHAPTER FOUR
PROGRESS

Dear Drew,
I'm taking this journey one day at a time,
learning to navigate my heartbreak.
Love, Mom

AS WE HURRIED THROUGH the preschool parking lot in the desert chill, I barely registered the biting wind on my exposed skin. We were on our way to Devin's holiday performance, the first after Drew's death, and Joey wanted to get a good seat. After we settled, the curtains pulled back, and I could almost hear the audience hold its collective breath as thirty nervous preschoolers wearing their holiday finest arranged themselves onstage. Their sheepish smiles and shuffling feet fell into place, and with a silent cue from the teacher, a chorus of tiny angelic voices filled the multipurpose room. I looked around at all the parents melting with pride and adoration. Joey was the picture of joy. As I stared at my beloved boy onstage, I suddenly realized I felt nothing at all.

I had been on carefully prescribed mood-supporting medications since shortly after Drew's passing. Along with therapy and self-care, the medications allowed me to return to daily life. They had lessened the pain and suffering by a degree, and I had progress to show. I did not struggle as much to take Devin to school or cook dinner or meet up with a friend. I'd even taken some of Drew's old toys out of the closet for Devin and me to play with. When I inevitably teared up, Devin would ask why I was sad, to which I could now reply: "I'm not sad, sweetheart. I'm remembering. These are happy tears." In those moments, I was starting to access a tentative sense of gratitude. Though Drew's life was brief, it was real. Our love for him was as undeniable as the Thomas the Tank Engine in Devin's hands. So instead of thinking about Drew's absence, I practiced remembering the moments when both of my boys would be hysterically laughing in their secret, imagined world. I wasn't free from the pain of those triggers by any means, but they gained more nuance, tinged with the recognition of Drew's beautiful life.

While the difficult moments were becoming more than solely difficult, as I sat in that multipurpose room, I knew the joyful moments were becoming less joyful—the joy replaced by a cloudiness I couldn't rise above even when I wanted to. Yes, the medication gave me the ability to function, but it also cost me my ability to feel anything positive. I didn't want to hurt, but if not hurting also meant surrendering all joy, then I was willing to face the pain. After all, I didn't have peace; I had numbness. The pain was still there, just suppressed. While I needed the numbness for a time, I also knew I was ready to feel more. Slowly. Cautiously. But more.

That same Christmas we went to my mom's house for dinner. I walked in and immediately noticed that all the pictures of Drew were gone. None hung on the walls or sat on the mantle. No pictures of him anywhere. Nothing.

I freaked out.

Some days I felt like I made progress in processing my grief; other days, I felt like all that progress was stripped away in an instant by a trigger I never saw coming. I knew my mom never intended harm, but it was as though she had erased Drew from our family. I couldn't lose Drew and his memory too. When I finally calmed enough to ask my mom about it, she said she had taken down his photos because she thought it would hurt me too much to see them. What she didn't know was that to me, Drew's memory was everything. It was all I had left.

After that Christmas, my mom helped me hang photos of Drew all over the house. People would come over and say, "Wow, he's everywhere." *Exactly.* They might see the photos and think I was stuck in the past or unable to move on, but the photos made me feel happy, connected. Avoiding Drew hurt so much more. Finally, I had started to grieve with intention—and that progress sustained me.

We must reframe how we think about healing and how we measure progress in the healing process.

It is tempting to try to fit the healing experience into a neat little package. We want it to be a one-and-done process, no loose ends. After all, it would be much simpler to approach emotional wounds like items to check off a to-do list. But healing isn't static or formulaic. It is rarely solved in one go because the process changes and evolves as we do. To make our way through this process with less confusion and unnecessary pain, we must reframe some of the misconceptions about how we heal. These reframes may not take root immediately. You may feel a knee-jerk reaction to rail against them. That's fine. We will explore these concepts in more depth throughout this book, and it takes practice to integrate them into everyday life. But they will inspire the clarity and courage needed to create momentum on the healing journey.

Emotional healing requires intention and effort.

Some kinds of healing are automatic. If you tear a nail beneath the quick, painful as it is, you don't have to do anything to make the nail regrow. If you have surgery, you may have to care for the wound, but you don't have to consciously think about the incision for it to mend; with time and rest, it will close on its own. Physical healing is, in part, dependent on time.

Emotional healing, on the other hand, is much more dependent on intention, choice, and effort. Time may create distance from emotional pain, which can aid the healing process, but it doesn't typically create healing on its own. Traumatic memories can stay gaping wounds forever if we don't actively treat them. Emotional healing comes with intentional effort, extended practice, and loving patience.

Healing happens in layers and iterations.

Though it can be maddening for us more logical types, healing is rarely a linear process. The pace often feels jerky and inconsistent, like a teenager learning to drive, and it might seem like you're going in circles instead of taking the most direct route. Sometimes you need to learn the same lesson three, four, or five times before you can integrate it into your life in a meaningful way. While that will cause some inherent frustration, it will not likely change.

You can, however, change your mindset to lean into the process and create more ease. Each time a trigger or difficult emotion comes up, try to greet it like an old friend and look for the information it has to share, the lesson it has to teach. Rather than criticizing yourself for not getting it right the first (or fifteenth) time, practice giving yourself grace and, without judgment, ask yourself: What more can I learn here?

Healing happens at your own pace.

You don't have to take on everything at once. Trying to do so will overwhelm you and cause more stress than peace. Think of toddlers learning to walk; they aren't born with the ability to compete in an Ironman. It takes years, not to mention parental guidance, to learn to get up on all fours, crawl, walk, and run, let alone build enough endurance to compete in a triathlon. The image of toddlers running, swimming, and biking their way through an Ironman is laughable.

Likewise, we can't expect ourselves to complete the equivalent of an emotional Ironman without significant time, effort, and support. When you feel like you are in over your head, remember that *you* get to decide what and how much you take on. *You* are in control of this journey. Some dynamics and patterns will be harder to shift than others, so it is important to remember that any step is a positive step. You can go as fast or as slow as you want, but progress is dependent on your daily choice to do *something*.

Healing is messy because you are trying new things.

The healing process is a learning process. Maybe you try to implement tool after tool, each designed to create more inner peace, but none of them work for you. So you let them go. Then, almost as if by accident, you stumble upon something that does work, so you hold onto it. When things finally feel good, you backslide, or a trigger comes out of nowhere. You put up a boundary, and someone lashes out at you. The friction of change starts to wear on you.

Healing feels messy. Sometimes you might be tempted to look at the mess and say, "I'd rather not deal with this. Let's call someone to haul it away." Wouldn't it be nice if life worked like that? But catastrophic failures—and trust me, I've had plenty—are still progress. Even in my meltdowns, I still became more aware of my triggers. By tuning into what was happening internally, I learned to stop myself from unraveling with less effort and more grace. I made less mess. My healing felt more productive, focused, and deliberate, but it happened only when I accepted the mess instead of fighting it. If your healing feels messy, that is a clear sign of progress.

Progress is measured by effort, not completion.

The messy, uncertain, and iterative nature of the healing process can be more than a little frustrating—like losing at Chutes and Ladders. You climb your way to the top of the board game, one rung at a time, until you're a ladder away from a critical breakthrough. *Boom*—a trigger sends you riding that chute back to where you started. You thought you were a climb away from putting the game behind you, and now you're left wondering if all that effort was worth it. Confused and defeated, you wonder whether you are even making progress.

Remember when you were in school and kids would mockingly say "A for effort" to signify that you actually failed? In the healing game, effort really is the win. Every rung counts. It still counts when you climb a few steps and then slide right past them ten minutes later—because you learned by exerting the effort. A setback can be transformed into a "setup" when you approach it the right way. After a chute, there's always another ladder waiting on your next turn; you just have to keep playing to access it. Progress is measured in the insights you learn along the way, as well as your willingness to put those lessons into daily practice. You grow from the effort required by the task, not only by completing it.

When you're tempted to negate all your headway, search for signs of progress—and realize they might look different from what you initially expected. For example, some examples of healing "metrics" might be:

- You experience your triggers differently, even if your response to them doesn't change quite yet. (In fact, when this happens, you might be close to a breakthrough.)
- You repeat the same mistake three times, but your recovery time gets shorter and less challenging with each go.
- You move through challenging events, emotions, or days more quickly and with less energy.
- The time you spend licking your wounds after a fight is shortened because you have had to pick yourself up enough times to know that you can come back from anything.

Other signs of progress can include fewer triggering situations, less painful triggers, more moments of awareness, more moments of clarity, a sense of control, acts of self-compassion, feelings of pride or contentedness after facing tough situations, lightened symptoms of depression and anxiety, and a sense that you're better able to handle whatever comes next. Even the simple act of being aware of the need to heal is progress.

By staying open and curious about your progress, you can create the forward momentum needed to carry you through the tougher parts of the journey.

THE HEALING PROCESS IS NEVER TRULY DONE.

Decades into my healing journey, what I know for sure is that healing is never truly done. It might be trite, but it's true: Healing is not a destination; it's a journey. When we experience profound loss, like the loss of a child, the pain does not simply disappear with time; it becomes a part of who we are. Healing involves learning how to carry that pain, finding ways to live alongside it, and discovering moments of joy and growth despite and because of it.

As we grow, new layers of our experience emerge. Events like milestones and anniversaries and merely the passage of time can bring new perspectives to our loss and our healing. What felt like closure one year may feel tender again the next. Healing is a lifelong process of adapting, understanding, and finding meaning.

While the endless nature of emotional healing might sound like a burden, I choose to view it as the one area of my life where I always get a do-over. There are some losses—like Drew's accident—for which no do-over is ever possible. But in healing from those losses, you get as many attempts as you need and want.

I don't want to make it seem like healing is easy—take the lemons and make lemonade. Sometimes the lemon squirts juice in your eye. But if your healing process hasn't been as simple as following a step-by-step guide, that is verifiable proof that you are well on your way to healing. If it feels rocky and chaotic at times, you are doing it *right*. Healing is a beautifully messy, unique, and imperfect journey. So let it be.

What Helped Me: Internal Check-Ins

Healing progress can be small and incremental, and without intentionally carving out time and space to notice it, you might miss it. Internal check-ins are regular, dedicated times for reflection that encourage you to search for and recognize new measures of progress. I'll share my process as a model so you can try it, or you can find your own approach.

I like to choose the same time each week to be alone in a safe, comfortable space. I usually start with a body scan, meditation, or prayer. I often set an intention for the practice so I know what I want to get out of it. For instance, I might identify a particular relationship or situation that needs attention. I might ask myself how I feel physically and mentally. Then I sit with my feelings and see what comes up.

If you have a journal, you might find it helpful to bring it into this practice. Your journal is a history of your progress and evolution in healing. Sometimes you can literally see the progress in your handwriting. In the earliest days of my loss, my writing was erratic, big, and filled with exclamation points and violent underlines—an illustration of the magnitude of my feelings. But when I flipped through the pages months later, I could see the progression into something more fluid and methodical, with the clarity of a period instead of the uncertainty of an ellipsis. By keeping and looking back at journals, we can create opportunities to feel proud of our growth.

Being able to intentionally pull back and focus on the most compassionate view of your journey is incredibly powerful. Internal check-ins are an especially useful tool for those moments of challenge or doubt when you don't know what you're thinking or feeling, when you feel lost on your journey, or when you fear you're failing or falling behind.

Progress isn't always celebrated with a cheer or a pat on the back, but pausing to see the distance you have come sure feels good and can fuel your continuing steps.

CHAPTER FIVE
ACCEPTANCE

Dear Drew,
The way you'd curl up in my lap during story time,
your head resting against my chest,
is a moment I relive often.
Love, Mom

WHEN DREW DIED, I knew he was never coming back. I had watched the groundskeepers place his casket in the mausoleum on that stifling afternoon in May. But like many people after a significant loss, I didn't know how to accept the finality of it. And more importantly, I didn't want to. So for a long time, I allowed my mind to engage in "magical thinking." I entertained the belief that Drew *hadn't* died. He was like Peter Pan, the boy who would never grow up, off on grand adventures in Neverland.

One night a few weeks after Drew's funeral, as I sat at my desk with my journal, I started writing a letter to Drew in Neverland. I knew he couldn't write me back, but each word felt like it connected me to him across time and space. When I was done, I closed my journal and set it on my windowsill, imagining that Drew would fly in while I slept and read the words I never got to say to him.

My dearest Drewby,

Where you are, can you hop from cloud to cloud? When you land, is it like cotton candy? Can you pull the different flavor clouds apart with your always-sticky fingers?

Love, Mama

I wrote a letter to Neverland every night for the first year after Drew's passing. I was desperate to alleviate my pain, but I didn't want to do that by forgetting Drew or pushing him away. I needed a different way to *be* with him. Every time I sat down to write a letter, I was with him, and I freed myself from a little bit of the hurt and blame and pain. I worked a lot of things out on those pages—all the things I wanted to say to him, all the magical thoughts I wished could be true—as I emptied out the sadness to make room for hope. The letters to Neverland were my way of arriving in reality at my own speed. They were my safe space, just beyond the bounds of reality, where I could briefly escape from the finality of Drew's loss—because it was so immense I couldn't have accepted it all at once. Each time I scratched "Dear Drew" onto a fresh page, I was giving myself the permission to take my time.

Even with the worried warnings from loved ones in my ear, I somehow understood that I needed to be patient with myself. There were times over the first year that I felt impatient and a little scared with what I was allowing. *Why can't you stop feeling this way? Can't you see you're losing your grip like everyone says?* But when I could silence those voices and return to my journal, I knew I was processing the very emotions I needed to feel to finally arrive at acceptance.

As the first anniversary of Drew's passing crept closer, I could sense a shift coming. Every time I faced my feelings on the page, I was one step closer to accepting the loss. That meant I was also getting closer to leaving Neverland behind. At some point, Drew had to stop being Peter Pan, and I needed to allow for the reality that my son had passed. I had sat with the pain and escaped it in equal measure. For a time, Neverland was a tender mercy. But now I had to plant my feet firmly on the ground again if I wanted any chance at moving forward. Otherwise, I ran the risk of getting lost in Neverland forever—when Drew was never there in the first place. I had to find a new way to make his life feel like it was still a part of mine.

WE MUST ACCEPT OUR PAIN AND OUR PROCESS WITHOUT JUDGMENT, OR WE RUN THE RISK OF BECOMING LOST OR STUCK ON THE HEALING JOURNEY.

Accepting a painful reality can feel extremely threatening to the mind and body, even when we know we cannot change it. Magical thinking was my heart's way of sidestepping the threat and feeling safe again, on a timeline that was gentle enough for me to traverse willingly and lovingly. It takes time to learn that accepting a loss does not mean leaving our loved one behind—and that it is still possible to nurture a connection while accepting that they're gone. But acceptance doesn't happen all at once; it is a layered process.

First, we must accept where we are at any given moment. Maybe you are heartbroken, scared, and flailing—unsure of how to carry on. Maybe you had a picture of how your life would look right now or how you "should" be feeling. Let go of those expectations. Let wherever you are be enough; however far you have come is enough.

Then, we must accept that, possibly, there is a different way to move through an experience than the way we have been trying. Pushing too hard, forcing the process, or fighting against it only makes it worse. Sometimes, we must surrender. I don't mean collapse; I mean lean into the process and whatever is happening in it, illogical though it may seem at times (like visiting a storybook world).

Eventually, we must also accept our responsibility in moving through the pain to find acceptance. It was up to me to decide when and how I would face the finality of my loss. That was the beginning of my work on acceptance—of my loss, of the journey ahead, of my role in shaping it. Years later, I would also work on self-acceptance. You too must find your own path to acceptance, starting where you are now.

As if the process of acceptance isn't hard enough, judgment surrounds it: Your grief must fit into five stages, follow a certain timeline, and be palatable enough for other people to watch. Everyone else has their own idea about what grief should look like, despite the fact that it is not theirs to carry. They can see *your* pain only from *their* perspective. Few take the time to stop and ask what the griever believes about their pain and what they need to move through it. But if we don't process grief in our own way, then we'll likely get stuck trying to move through it according to others' expectations. We must accept that the grieving process is meant to be as unique as the griever, and it never deserves judgment—from yourself or others.

With grief, there is no right or wrong answer. There is no single way through it. There's just the way that works for you. You are in charge of your journey to reach acceptance.

What Helped Me: Journaling

Journaling has been used as a therapeutic tool for processing trauma for decades. Not only can writing about traumatic experiences help with processing emotions more effectively, but it can also reduce symptoms of depression, anxiety, and PTSD in trauma survivors. By emptying our thoughts onto the page, we can confront our emotions in a controlled manner, with less emotional distress over time. In fact, recent studies using functional MRI have shown that expressive writing can lead to changes in brain activity associated with emotional processing and regulation. This supports the idea that journaling can help reframe traumatic experiences and integrate them into our life story in an intentional way.

While journaling can sometimes feel frustrating or intimidating, especially when confronting a traumatic event, it doesn't have to fit any specific formula. The trick is to find the approach that feels good to you. If you need to write about a fantastical world for a year, do it. If sending letters to an empty mailbox works, then go right ahead. Poetry, songwriting, and screenplays are also on the table. Play and experiment until something clicks, until you find yourself being pulled to the page. But don't overlook the healing power of putting pen to paper.

CHAPTER SIX
AGENCY

Dear Drew,
Each sunrise brings new chances
to remember you and seek the light.
Love, Mom

IN THE MONTHS AFTER DREW'S ACCIDENT, I did all the things I thought I needed to do to heal from his loss. I went to therapy multiple times a week. I took medication under the care of my doctors. I worked closely with the local clergy to try to answer my questions of faith. I developed a tolerance for the tasks of daily life and interacting with the world, and I got back into my normal routines.

Fast-forward a few years, and to most of the world I probably looked fine. Fully recovered. Heck, I even had my counselors, family, and friends convinced I felt better. But the truth is, I was merely going through the motions so I could say I was doing the work. I realized that if I stayed busy, surrounded myself with friends, filled my calendar with social events and parties, volunteered at Devin's school, and worked ridiculous hours, I could distract myself from the pain and hide from what I felt. Soon I began to live for those moments of artificial relief. When I did have free time, I tried to fill the void of my loss with spending sprees, cramming my closet and house with pretty things in an effort to find reasons to smile. *If I'm smiling, then I'm okay . . . right?*

I played this game for years, creating the illusion of healing and happiness. But when no one else was looking, I spent every breath quieting the voice inside my head that reminded me if I hadn't fallen asleep that day, Drew would still be alive, Devin would be playing with him, and my marriage would be strong. The cracks were beginning to show, my perfectly put-together facade crumbling.

One morning I woke up and thought, *I am sick and tired of feeling so sick and tired.* No matter how hard I tried to run from it or deny it, when I turned out the lights at night, I was as overwhelmed by my pain as ever. Back at the same crossroads again, I turned to the one person I felt truly understood me.

This time when I read Theresa's letter, a different sentence grabbed me by the chest: *If you choose to find happiness and joy, it will be there for you.* As I ran my palm over the letter's creases, tracing the ink with my fingertips, I couldn't let go of three words: *If you choose.* I remember the thought struck me like the answer to a test I didn't know I was taking: *Oh, I get to decide?*

Something inside me shifted. *Hold on a minute, if I get to decide, then I don't choose this. If I get to decide, then I want to be okay again. If I get to decide, then I choose to believe I am still worthy of a healed, fulfilled, meaningful, purpose-driven life. If I get to decide, from now on, I choose more than* this.

A light turned back on in my soul.

For years, I had chosen false forms of happiness, surface-level healing, and quick fixes to my pain. And they didn't work: I was just as destroyed as the day I lost Drew.

If I had a choice, though, then I could still choose differently. This time, I would choose to face the pain I had been running from—no matter what.

TO FIND EMPOWERMENT IN PAIN, WE MUST RECOGNIZE AND SEIZE THE MOMENT OF AGENCY.

Our lives are defined by the moments of agency we see and don't see. Our happiness is shaped by the choices we make and avoid. It is in these choices—and in our ability to embrace them as personal power—that healing and thriving can be created. What heals us is not time, numbing, avoiding, distracting, withdrawing, or escaping. It is choice.

You choose when to heal. You choose how to heal. *You choose.*

When you work for an organization, in order to bind the company contractually, you must be given agency. In your own life, you already have agency. No one needs to give it to you—it is yours.

There is enormous value in owning our choices, yet I see many people give away their agency every day. "Oh, no, you decide. You pick. It's your choice." But I know my answers. Where do you want to go for dinner? Giuseppe's. Where would you go on a dream vacation? Scotland. What's the meaning of life? To see my experiences as opportunities to create good in this world.

Today, I know what I choose, and I rarely give up my agency, whether it is something as inconsequential as dinner or as fundamental as the meaning of my own life. I would go so far as to say that the thing I love most about life is that I *do* get to choose. I love knowing that I am the one who creates my experience. For the next ten minutes, ten days, or ten years, I get to have an impact on how my life goes and what it means. It feels empowering to understand that I get a say—that I get the *ultimate* say.

Early in grief, it is easy to rail against the idea that we can choose to heal. When something terrible happens, it is tempting to scream, "I didn't ask for this! I didn't choose this. Why should I have to carry the burden of healing from it too?" I understand. I do. I would never have chosen for my son to die in an accidental drowning, but at some point, I had to choose to heal, or I would lose myself to anguish. Choosing to take on the challenge of healing means accepting that the pain is yours. But the very act of choosing to see your pain, and then doing the work to heal from it, is what sets you free from the burden of carrying it. It is not fair or easy, but making that choice is where your power begins.

• • •

Agency means living by choice or by consequence. When we live by choice, we make decisions with intention and awareness; we take action and ownership at every possible opportunity; we are the author of our own story. We cannot stop adversity from touching our lives, but we do not have to succumb to it either. When we live by consequence, we become passive bystanders, handing over the pen to whoever wants control of the ending.

This idea of living by choice might seem odd, or obvious, or maybe incomprehensible, but it is a crucial piece of the puzzle that takes intentional practice.

First, we must recognize the moment of agency. When reeling from fresh pain or numb from years of enduring it, we can struggle to see the moment of agency in front of us. We often feel like we have no choice at all when we may actually have many. They might not be the choices we want. They might not be good choices. But they are there. When someone criticizes or demeans us, the way we respond is a choice. What we believe about ourselves and others is a choice. How we think about our options is a choice. In Viktor Frankl's classic *Man's Search for Meaning,* about his time as a prisoner in a Nazi concentration camp, he writes, "Everything can be taken from a man but one thing: the last of the human freedoms—to choose one's attitude in any given set of circumstances, to choose one's own way." Though Frankl could control almost nothing about his circumstances, he could choose how he responded to them.

No matter what you have endured, that choice exists for you too. Even when you choose not to address something, you are still choosing. Not to decide is to decide, so you might as well reflect on your options and consider what it would look like to choose the path that is in your best interest. What decision will help you create the outcome you desire? What outcome supports you with compassion and growth?

For me, "good" choices move in the direction of my vision and goals; I feel proud when I make them (especially the hard ones). When I let anger, frustration, and hurt overrun my level head and open heart, I am more likely to make "bad" choices, so I practice asking:

- Which choices align with my personal value system?
- Which choices allow for the most possibility?
- Even though an option may seem impossible, what could be possible if I chose it?

Doing so allows me to think clearly, choose with my highest self, and commit to my decision. The decision is instrumental because everything follows from that point. We must be clear on the choice to be clear on what comes next. Then, we must *act* on that choice.

Agency requires deliberate and consistent action, which, when sustained over time, gives you a sense of empowerment. For instance, you might learn something that can help you heal, such as the power of meditation in managing overwhelming thoughts. You can read studies, decipher the science, and hear firsthand accounts about how meditation has helped others. But until you decide to meditate regularly—and act on that choice every day—you have not yet tapped into your agency. Agency is both Frankl's ability to choose his attitude in horrendous circumstances *and* his actions to live that attitude.

Everything you choose leads toward either healing or a continuation of where you are, and healing requires that you choose it every day. Choosing how to think, be, and behave is not easy, but it is necessary. So choose to believe that healing is possible. Choose to see the moments of agency that might be obscured by your pain. Choose to believe you are capable and worthy of more. Then commit and recommit to the healing process until you actually feel better. Start small, practice, and then take a slightly bigger step. But do not stop. Do not give up. When you fall two steps back, make the conscious choice to acknowledge the stumble but also to believe you are capable of moving forward again. Embrace your agency.

What Helped Me: Agency Reflection

The ability to recognize moments of agency in daily life is a skill that most of us need to learn and develop throughout the healing process. We are not born knowing how to do it (or if we are, we unlearn it quickly), and we don't all grow up with strong role models. We must learn through practice. Agency is a crucial concept, and we will build on the idea throughout this book. If you need practice seeing your moments of agency, you might find, as I did, that a daily agency reflection can help. Here's how you might approach it:

At the end of each day, choose an environment that makes you feel safe and open to observation and curiosity rather than judgment. In your journal, answer these questions:
- Where did you notice your agency today?
- Where did you *not* feel a sense of agency?
- How did you exercise your agency?
- What were the outcomes of your choices?
- What has changed over time?

Meet the answer to each question with compassion, and you will reach more truthful answers.

PART TWO

Acquire New Tools

GRIEF UPROOTS YOUR WORLD in unimaginable ways, leaving you unsteady and unprepared for the sprawling landscape of life after loss. The tools you once relied on to make sense of your inner world now splinter in your hands. Tending to the nuances of grief requires softness and fortitude in equal measure, so you must protect yourself or risk further injury. A little dirt under the fingernails won't hurt, but the goal is not to create more wounds each time you dig into unruly earth.

    This work might feel daunting, even dangerous, but I will not send you into rough terrain unequipped. Before you lower to hands and knees, I will remind you to slip on your protective gloves and reach for new tools: a sturdy trowel for loosening what feels unmovable, a pruner for cutting away what no longer serves you, a watering can for nourishment when grief asks too much. Cultivation asks you to be flexible, trading one tool for the next as the weather shifts or new pests find your tender undergrowth.

I am here, a witness to your toil. While I can sit next to you among the buried memories, fears, and dreams, I cannot choose your tools for you or place them in your hands. You must pick them up and practice, learning with each till. I urge you to look beyond the conventional set of tools. Sift through the soil with a spoon until you can wield the shovel and throw your body into the digging. This is your earth to tend. Trust that wildflowers grow where beauty and chaos meet.

Then start digging.

CHAPTER SEVEN
INNER VOICE

Dear Drew,
I can still hear your laughter and
feel your warmth in the quiet moments.
Love, Mom

FOR MONTHS, I had been diligent about doing the work—the real work, not the surface work. But I felt like I was barely making progress and certainly not fast enough. As I walked into a counseling session, my impatience had swelled into agitation.

Sensing frustration, my therapist asked me what was going on, and when I opened my mouth, I surprised myself with what I said: "There's so much *noise*. The pain is still the only thing I can hear. I can feel it reverberating in every cell of my being. I'm still setting my timer every day to intentionally think about the happy moments, and I can hear that quiet, compassionate voice in the back of my mind say, *Give yourself fifteen minutes of peace. You can do that. It will be okay.* But my critical voice is still there when the timer stops. It's like when you turn up the volume on the TV because you don't want to hear what someone has to say. I can either turn up the volume and drown out both voices, or I can turn it down and let them wage war inside me. I feel desperate for a moment of internal peace because I'm *exhausted*. It requires so much effort to block out or avoid what I'm terrified to hear myself say, and I can't do it anymore!"

We sat in silence for a moment, my desperate plea hanging in the space between us like an echo.

"Why don't you journal it out?" he suggested.

I knew he was going to say that. But that day, I did not want to accept my place in the healing process. I wanted it to be over. *Give me the magic pill. Tell me the answer. Do you have any idea how far I've come? And I'm still miles from where I want to be.* I couldn't confront the length of road that lay ahead. It was too much.

I don't know what came over me, but I looked at my therapist with all the rage and despair I'd been hiding and said, "I am so sick of you telling me to *journal it out*. I am not doing that. It is not helping with this throbbing tangle of pain in my chest." I flailed my hands wildly in front of my chest, pausing to look at him. "And if you tell me to write one more time, I'm going to throw my journal at your head!"

No reaction.

"Well, go on—tell me to breathe one more time. I'll lose my freaking mind! I can't sit calmly and act like this is okay anymore. I've got to *move* this pain!"

"What if you tried dancing or kickboxing—physical movement?" he offered, still steady and calm.

"That's not what I mean!" *I'll have to show you.*

I wrenched my journal out of my purse, threw open the pages, and started scribbling. And I felt . . . better.

CHAPTER 7: INNER VOICE

I continued marring the pages until that stuck, frenetic pain released. Once there were enough scratches on the page that I had torn through to the next, I had finally created the visual representation of what I felt inside. I looked up, panting, slightly undone, definitely deranged, pleading for the answer.

Then, like the whisper of a soft breeze, I heard it: *You need to paint again.*

Our inner voice provides important messages and insights.

To paraphrase Carl Jung, what we resist persists. When we reject negative feelings or thoughts, they amplify.

Pretending not to hear the critical voice in my head only made it louder. I tried everything I could to suppress it, but I found no true sense of relief until I finally sat down and said, "Let me hear you." Those damaging thoughts and beliefs had to be disrupted—but not through suppression or denial or self-hatred or punishment. If I wanted to survive the noise in my head, I would have to start listening.

The Two Facets of Our Inner Voice

When we open ourselves up to hearing what is inside, we are typically met with *two* voices: one that feels loud and critical, and one that speaks softly with compassion. The conversation between them is what I call our inner voice.

The critical voice is the voice of the mind. It is loud, fast-paced, persistent, and distracting. It rationalizes everything we feel into a story, behavior, or reaction meant to protect us. Because its logic is persuasive, this voice is easily confused with truth. *If only you had prepared better, you would not have failed. If only you were smarter, you would have done it right.* It will criticize us to the point we become our own worst enemy. Since the critical voice is most often driven by fear and trauma, it makes sure we never forget a failure or misstep. The mind can tell us things that are not true, and because it is "rational," it is incredibly convincing.

The compassionate voice with its murmurs of encouragement and grace comes from the heart. It nudges us to dream bigger, listen to our intuition, follow our gut, and go our own way. It offers thoughts and ideas that lead toward more joy, passion, growth, and expansion. *Mistakes are part of the learning process; you can't grow without making mistakes. Beating yourself up does not make you better; supporting yourself does.* It is that all-knowing feeling that most of us have taught ourselves to ignore. The voice of the heart encourages us to find and share the contributions that only we have for this world. It is meant to guide us and give shape to our lives, even if the path seems impractical to our rational mind and to other people. Most importantly, the heart is always kind, always edifying. It is our personal source of unconditional love. It is where I finally heard the divine part of me, and it is where healing lies.

When we have the awareness to distinguish the two voices, the mind's criticisms begin to quiet long enough for the heart's voice to make itself heard. Then, suddenly, we start making discoveries. There is a strength, a resilience inside the enlightened heart that makes it possible to quiet our fears and invite a conversation between heart and mind. While the mind offers intellect, the heart holds limitless wisdom. By fostering a dialogue between the two, we can hear the intellect of the mind without the punishing aspects of our critical voice. We can ask: How can I harness my reasoning and align it with my heart? How can I bring in new knowledge while still trusting myself to know what to do with it? The conversation of our inner voice becomes a collaborative dance. The two voices no longer compete. They don't punish or wage war. The voices of the heart and mind work together to create a coherence that guides us forward with loving support rather than harsh criticism. We begin to tap into the truth of who we are—untouched by the painful events of our lives—and we are allowed to just be.

Figure 1 is a diagram of how I think about the inner voice: the critical and compassionate voices that create our full inner voice dialogue, the personal growth and emotional healing that can come from that dialogue, and the self-understanding that results.

Figure 1. The inner voice.

When our heart and mind cooperate, here's what our internal dialogue starts to sound like when, for instance, we make a mistake:

Okay, that didn't go how I hoped. It stings.

But I can acknowledge the disappointment without tearing myself apart. Mistakes happened, yes, but they don't define me.

I prepared the best I could with what I had at the time. And I can look at what worked and what didn't—without shame. This is part of learning, part of growing.

People might have noticed, and that's uncomfortable. But most are too focused on their own lives to judge as harshly as I fear. And even if they do, their judgment doesn't determine my worth.

What matters now is how I choose to respond. I can take responsibility without falling into self-punishment. I can adjust, grow, and show up better next time.

This moment is a chance, a reminder, and an invitation to treat myself with honesty and kindness.

I don't need to be perfect. I just need to be present.

And from here, I move forward with courage, clarity, and compassion.

Over time, this internal dialogue becomes more than just comforting—it becomes transformational. That's where personal growth takes root as we stop fighting ourselves and start evolving with intention. As we learn to meet pain with empathy instead of avoidance and punishing narratives, emotional healing follows. And through it all, we build self-understanding, not as something we figure out once, but as a way of living: curious, grounded, and in constant conversation with our truest self.

Tuning In to Your Inner Voice

When your inner and outer worlds are so loud, how do you tune in to your inner voice? It takes time, practice, and trust. But once you give it a try, that little voice inside you will become stronger and louder each day. Try some of these techniques to help you find the right frequency.

Journaling. Listening to your inner voice is not something to do merely when you want answers. It is something to do regularly and with dedication. Though journaling wasn't always the best tool to help me hear my inner voice, I turned to it often (when I didn't feel like throwing my journal, of course). Writing helps keep communication lines open on a consistent basis, and the haptic experience can reveal something truly special. Writing by hand connects us to a deeper, more intuitive part of ourselves that holds answers our minds and mouths (and keyboards) alone can't access. Freewriting—writing without purpose, structure, or intention—can help us dump thoughts and feelings onto the page in a cathartic way. I find it to be especially helpful when I am feeling confused, funky, or stuck. Writing prompts can also help spark new ideas, and throughout the book I will suggest various prompts and reflections. Take a look at the high-yielding questions below as well, and if you need more ideas, visit my website (melissahull.com) or try searching online for "writing prompts for emotional healing."

High-yielding questions. Honest self-reflection can be a powerful way to access your inner voice and have those tough internal conversations you've been shying away from. Sometimes asking yourself the right question is all you need for clarity to come flooding in. However, not all questions are created equal, and the quality of the question will determine the quality of the answer. Especially when you're addressing loss, *why* questions are typically focused on the past and lead us to the same information we have already. There will never be an answer that satisfies the question "Why my son?" I had to learn to stop asking it because *why* was the mental cyclone that uprooted all the what-ifs and threw all the could-have-beens directly into my path. Eventually, *why* started to feel like an addiction that robbed me of my stability and progress. For every step forward, a *why* question could send me ten steps back.

Instead, I learned to focus on questions that would yield new and useful information. Most often, those questions started with *what, where, when,* and *how.*

- What helps me connect to my inner voice?
- Where do I feel most at peace?
- When do I feel most connected to my intuition?
- How can I spend more time in supportive environments?

These questions propel us forward, especially when paired with journaling.

Meditation. While the quiet stillness of meditation is a powerful way to slow your thoughts and step back from the world, it can also help you connect with your true essence. For me, meditation helps move beyond cognitive thinking to access a deeply intuitive, all-knowing spiritual side of myself. In this space, I hear the whisperings of inner wisdom and even God. Practiced from a spiritual perspective, meditation offers a reprieve from pain, confusion, and fear—a place where the weight of life can melt away, no matter what you're facing.

For many people, the *how* of meditation is the trickiest part. There are many different styles to explore, but here's a simple guide to start:

CHAPTER 7: INNER VOICE

1. Sit comfortably in a quiet place.
2. Set a time limit.
3. Focus on your breath.
4. Notice your body and any sensations.
5. Relax your mind; notice any thoughts that arise, and then let them pass.

Be flexible with the duration of each meditation; you might start with three minutes and build gradually to thirty. Don't push too hard; allow yourself to pause when needed. If quiet doesn't work for you, try a guided meditation (visit my website, melissahull.com, for recordings, or search online for "guided meditation" or "meditation apps"). If sitting doesn't work for you, try lying down or walking slowly. Instead of worrying about doing it "right" or practicing a specific style, do what works for *you*. Approach your practice with curiosity and maybe even some humor. After all, it is just that: a practice.

Environment. In the early days of my healing work, I thought I had to sit still and be quiet to hear my inner voice. But I struggled with the ultracalm vibes of a traditional meditation space, and sometimes, it made it *harder* to quiet my mind. I decided to try it my own way and realized I didn't heal in just one location. I didn't need a specific room or scented candle; I needed an environment that sparked my inner awareness and gave me a sense of empowerment while I worked through issues. Different healing environments served me best at different times—indoors, outdoors; moving, still—and my preferences changed over time. Certain environments I relied on daily in the early stages of healing I now visit only occasionally, and I continue to discover new spaces and places.

Regardless of where it is, the goal of a healing environment is to give yourself the physical, emotional, and spiritual space to check in with yourself and align your inner world with the future you want to create. You might like the ultracalm vibes of a dedicated meditation space with incense, but if you need to put running shoes on and hop on the treadmill, then do it. If you need to get in the kitchen and smell cookies baking, great. If you need to garden with your hands in the cold dirt, go do it. Find *your* healing environment.

Movement. Sitting quietly isn't the only way to hear our innate wisdom. Moving your body is one of the quickest ways to silence the inner critic and tune in to the truth inside you, so my therapist made a reasonable suggestion with dancing and kickboxing. My go-to now is tennis. When I play, I concentrate on hitting the target in front of me. Everything but the ball fades away, and soon I have fallen into the rhythm of chasing the ball around the court. The *thwack* of the racket, the squeak of rubber soles on asphalt, the grunt that escapes me when I lunge for a hit—they all bring me into the moment. Falling into the methodical rhythm of the game, I become present and can hear myself think. You might find the same with running or rowing, but it need not be sports. Try dancing, drawing, or walking—anything that shifts your focus from thinking to doing.

WHAT HELPED ME: CLARITY BREAKS

If the healing journey has you feeling overwhelmed, lost, or plain old scared, try taking a clarity break—a dedicated amount of time to clear your head and decide what your next step will be. At first, I did this organically. Whenever I felt like I was losing my grip, I would go to my art studio and run through the tools I had acquired for listening to my inner voice. Over time, I realized I needed to make the practice more regular, and I started carving out time each day. Now, I take a clarity break whenever I feel myself reaching an edge—if I feel exhausted, emotional, or like life isn't moving in the direction I envisioned.

Whether it is ten minutes, an hour, or a week, a clarity break is a great way to define what you need while creating the time and space to meet those needs. Use any of the inner voice tools we've discussed in this chapter, and tap into the self-care practices you have established for support. Give yourself permission to slow down without guilt or judgment.

Sometimes the best way to see the solution to a problem is to stop thinking about it so much. Instead, let it go, step away, and shake things up. Choose an activity you love, such as walking in nature, playing your favorite sport, making art, or going somewhere new. Get in touch with your creative side, and let yourself play a little. Most importantly, trust that the answers will come. You simply have to connect with the parts of yourself that hold them.

CHAPTER EIGHT
EXPRESSION

Dear Drew,
I miss the way you'd tug at my sleeve
to show me your latest crayon drawings.
Love, Mom

WHEN MY INNER VOICE whispered to me in the therapist's office, I had not picked up a paintbrush in almost three years. Now I began to see paintings in my mind regularly, and I stood in front of a blank canvas almost on a daily basis. While painting, I did not have to talk about my pain or think about it or "process" it in any verbal way. Instead, it poured from me like the color splashing onto the canvas. Rage ripped its way out of me brushstroke by brushstroke. My inner voice spoke in pigments and images. With a paintbrush in my hand, I could finally be present in the moment, and that presence allowed me to start shifting that throbbing tangle of pain in my chest.

I used every aspect of my craft to express what was trapped in my mind. The thickness of the paint illustrated the weight I carried without reprieve. The dark colors and shadows evoked the intensity of emotion that coursed through me. My tenebristic style revealed the sorrow and shame I concealed deep inside. My desolate, disarrayed internal world was reflected externally. I emptied a lifetime of pain from my mind, body, and soul—and everything became lighter.

Once I rediscovered my ability for creative expression, I began telling the story of my love and my loss one image at a time. The words *hurt* and *loss* never felt sufficient. They couldn't encompass everything I felt: the constant barrage of anxious thoughts, the heaviness around my heart, the haunting final images of Drew imprinted on my soul. When painting, I could share the thoughts and feelings I didn't want to say out loud. Creative expression became the language of my grief, allowing me to show what I could not explain. Color became my voice, and the canvas became my story.

As I produced more and more work, I decided to share it. To my surprise, galleries enthusiastically showed my paintings, and viewers connected to my work. Though an untrained artist, I somehow conveyed emotion through the movement of paint in a way that other people understood, and my work often sold out. My technique might not have been the strongest, but the voice was clear. My early pieces revealed anger and hurt; as I got those emotions out, lighter things came forward. To pour my heart onto the canvas and then receive recognition for what I had created was extremely validating. I felt *seen*.

At this point, I began to channel my pain into every form of expression I could think of: fine art, writing, reading, music, decorating my home. By exploring different kinds of self-expression, I learned what I had to say and what I needed to keep the story moving forward. Every form of expression was on the table as long as it felt good to me. And once I found the type of creative work that gave me a sense of fulfillment, I never stopped.

Art invites us to express the parts of our experience locked inside us.

To heal, we must face our emotional pain. Only when we face it can we understand what it has to tell us. But meeting our pain is not easy; in fact, it can be frightening. Creative expression lets us meet our emotions by knocking on the side door rather than ringing the front doorbell. The entrance is a little more approachable.

Of course many forms of creative expression use words—written poetry, spoken word poetry, essay, memoir—but you might find, as I did, that it is easier to face your emotions when you don't have to use words. In that case, try visual and tactile forms of expression. Scribble, draw, stab holes in your notebook, create something and then tear it up. Use a crayon or paintbrush. Gather found objects in your yard. Allow for whatever comes—express it, and don't worry so much about the form it takes. If you have a hard time, you might try images of some kind. My feelings grew so big and moved so fast that I needed to put them where I could see them immediately; when I saw they fit on a canvas, suddenly they weren't so enormous anymore.

Find a creative language that feels fluid to you. Explore different options, and practice creating for fun. Focus on a few brushstrokes before you attempt an entire painting. Go for a walk along a new route and snap a few photos. Take a one-afternoon pottery class. Allow each creative step to naturally lead to the next. Notice when you begin to follow your creative instincts without realizing it. Use your creative voice until it becomes clear and confident.

Creative healing work takes courage, but it might be more cathartic than you expect. It often feels much better to bring the darkest parts of you into the light than to keep them buried in the deepest corners of your mind. And when you finish a particular creative session, you can leave some of the emotion there; you can come back to it any time you want, but you do not have to carry it with you. The weight of grief will lessen over time. By expressing your hidden pain, you learn to let it go—and you start to feel free again.

My creative expression has evolved over the years, but I always pursue it, because for me that's where the magic happens. In creative work, I feel myself in flow. There is a form of inspiration and expression that feels almost divinely guided, and it can lead you to incredible experiences: You lose track of time. You never get tired. Obstacles disappear. Your creativity finds a way.

While I still paint, now I often paint as a way of checking in or giving my subconscious mind a playground. Art is less about unloading what I feel and more about exploration and finding what I want to say. However, the outcome is the same: Creative work allows me to connect with my inner visionary and communicate what's inside, unfiltered and flowing freely.

I urge you to take a chance on the artistic process. Play with Play-Doh. Sing onstage. Try a drum circle, flower arranging, or a daily dance party alone in your room. Whatever the form, express yourself. You never know where it might lead.

What Helped Me: Creativity Self-Reflection

If you have not felt the invigorating rush of divine creativity in a while, or ever, then I have a great way to find possibilities to explore. Pick up your journal and settle yourself in a comforting space, then answer these questions. They are designed to spark inspiration from the heart, so don't overthink your answers:

- When you think back to childhood and teenage years, how did you play and spend your time? What made you feel special?
- In your adult life and throughout your career, what do you keep returning to? When do you feel the most free?
- What themes do you see?

Then write a short list of creative actions you could take right now: Carve out time for brainstorming or research; grab a book you've had your eye on; pick up art supplies that make you feel inspired; or sign up for a class. Don't limit yourself to what others consider "art."

Finally, choose one thing to try. Contemplation is important, but clarity is often found in action. The point is to dip your toe into the creative waters and see where the temperature feels right. You can always change direction from there, but first you must begin.

CHAPTER NINE
ENERGY

Dear Drew,
The way you looked when you were
chasing bubbles still feels like magic to me.
Love, Mom

I HAD DIVED into my healing work with ferocity, and as it can sometimes do, talk therapy exacerbated some old wounds and memories as I worked through them. In between sessions, I struggled with increased anxiety, so my psychiatrist suggested going back on medication. But I had been tapping into my intuition more and more, and my inner voice told me that meds were not the answer. My therapist asked me if the medication would be a better solution than enduring the pain and anxiety.

"For the longest time, I would have said yes, but I don't think that's true anymore," I replied. "The emptiness I feel on medication has become scarier than the pain." I needed to feel the emotions to sort through them—but without such unchecked intensity.

My psychiatrist suggested I try practicing meditation to help with my anxiety. Meditation was my first introduction to anything that could be considered "alternative" healing. When I sat silently in my own company, something stirred within me. And it felt *good*. There was a comforting presence there, like I was reconnecting with a part of myself for the first time in a long time.

The more I leaned into meditation, the more I became curious about alternative healing, and I began exploring. I asked friends for recommendations, read books, and tried to remain open.

My first discovery was Healer's Blueprint, an energy healing program rooted in cellular energy release and led by Tam Pendleton. A unique blend of science, energy healing, meditation, and faith, the program made sense in my bones. "The subconscious mind runs the body and all memory. That memory is stored in every body cell," Pendleton writes. "If we clear the cells of any dysfunctional subconscious memory, we may clear habits and patterns of behavior that have been creating lifelong limiting beliefs." Using a guided meditation system, I found and then released trauma from where it was stored in my subconscious mind and body. Through this process, I "reset" the memory in my cells.

For so long, my spirit had lost its vibrance. When I looked into the mirror, I could see the dullness in my eyes. Cellular energy release felt like taking an eraser and removing all the crud that my life experiences had caked onto my soul. Layer by layer, I returned to my original "imprint"—the person I was created to be. The more I worked at this practice, the more I realized my imprint had always been there—I just couldn't see it when it was covered with crud. This form of healing felt like returning home to myself. Sure enough, one day I looked in the mirror and saw that renewed sparkle in my eyes.

As I started to understand more about my personality, history, and emotional blocks, it became easier to show myself compassion. Rather than condemning myself for crying during a tough conversation, I recognized that my sensitive nature and ability to sit in hard emotions was a strength. The energy work helped me remove some of the shame around the "negative" parts of my nature. Instead, I could stop and say, "That explains why I am like this! This is who I am—and it is okay. In fact, it's more than okay. It is good and right for me to be who I am."

By the time I discovered Reiki, I was *so* ready for the power and peace it restored to my body. An ancient Japanese technique, Reiki works with the *ki*, life force energy, to bring balance to the body's unseen energetic system. Someone can practice Reiki on you, or you can practice it on yourself. It typically involves the practitioner putting their hands on or near a part of the body to help the energy flow. Reiki is one of those alternative practices that has many skeptics, but it gave me the relief I had been hoping was possible since I first picked up Theresa's letter. I could *finally* feel the heaviness dissipating from my bones; my body felt truly at rest. After experiencing the benefit of Reiki, I pursued certification as a practitioner so I could help others experience it as well.

When I discovered Dr. David R. Hawkins's Map of Consciousness, it was the "aha" moment I was looking for. Using a scientifically validated logarithmic scale, Hawkins calibrated the frequencies of emotions, thoughts, and behaviors to develop a framework for understanding human consciousness. He then compiled twenty years of research and testing into a map of emotions and their correspondence to our levels of consciousness. Each emotion has a different energy and vibration, which he describes in detail and places on a scale of zero to one thousand, from shame, guilt, and apathy to joy, peace, and enlightenment.

When I looked at Hawkins's map, everything started to make sense for me. I realized my emotional world was keeping me chained to the bottom of the scale. But the map offered more than clarity—it provided a way out of the pain. If I used the scale to identify what I was feeling, then I could also pinpoint the next higher emotion and climb my way toward it. I began using Hawkins's map to navigate my emotional world. If I felt myself spiraling into a dark place, I would stop everything and take a moment to check in. Retreating to a private space, I used Hawkins's map and descriptions to guide myself toward a higher frequency.

If I felt shame, for example, I would identify the thought associated with that shame—*I'm a terrible mother*—and reverse it. Using a targeted positive affirmation—*I never intended to hurt my son; I loved my son, and I'm a caring, dedicated mother*—I could start to undo the damage of that highly traumatic thought. I was realigning with the *truth* instead of the *trauma*. If I continually turned a negative thought into a positive one, eventually my emotions followed suit. Over time, my emotions realigned, and I began to feel like a good mother again. I no longer had to convince myself it was true; it felt true. I was able to use Hawkins's map as a guide to identify and shift my emotions by choice.

At this point, Hawkins's research felt like a lifeline because I could trust its science, backed by evidence and data. By comparison, my trust in God felt tenuous. As I looked elsewhere for truth—science, energy work, mindful awareness—these practices felt safer than returning fully to my faith. It would take much more healing before I was ready to approach my spirituality with the same eagerness that I explored these alternative tools.

Each modality I studied was validated by the next, and I stopped questioning what I discovered. The methods were not mainstream, but it did not matter: They worked. With each new practice, I gained a deeper awareness of what I felt and why and how to adjust that feeling when needed. I gained tools for my healing toolbelt, which I put on with intention and consistency. Clumsily at first, I accessed and navigated my energy and emotions, gaining success with time and practice. I went on an energetic treasure hunt throughout my body where the prize was discovering the source of a lifelong trauma. While that may sound terrifying, it actually gave way to immense relief.

The trick: learning to sit with the discomfort. I paid attention when negative emotions or sensations arose within me—panic in my chest, sadness weighing heavy in my limbs. When I noticed these bodily sensations, I knew where to start. The work was hard but worth it. The energy healing process helped me find the origin of my pain so I could finally release it, relief opening me up like a breath of fresh air. Healing through energy work felt like a rediscovery of who I was, and over time, I could see how these practices provided me with a new ability to become the highest version of myself.

We must understand the energy of our emotions in order to choose them with intention.

The link between mind and body is well acknowledged. Breathing and mindfulness practices calm the nervous system, reducing anxiety and its physical symptoms, such as a racing heart. Laughing releases endorphins and boosts the immune system. Unprocessed emotions like grief or anger can contribute to chronic pain; addressing them can offer physical and emotional relief.

When we recognize how our bodies and minds work together through energy, we harness our inner power to heal trauma, and we learn to choose our desired emotional state, which, in a virtuous cycle, can elevate our physical health and well-being.

The Body as Recordkeeper

Residual trauma hides not only in our hearts and minds but also in our bodies. Everything we have experienced, even if we are not consciously aware of it, is recorded in our bodies. We store memories on a subconscious level, and our bodies calibrate to those experiences.

Have you ever returned to a location where trauma occurred and felt an overwhelming, visceral response in your mind and body? Your hands sweat, your pulse races, and suddenly you feel like you have been transported back to the original event. Your body remembers the sensory details of that location—sights, smells, sounds—and it triggers the trauma memory in your mind. That is what I am talking about. Our emotions leave a cellular imprint that our bodies cannot ignore.

When trauma occurs, the body activates the fight-or-flight response in the nervous system, and it releases certain chemicals that travel through our entire system and into our cells. This process changes the way our bodies respond to certain triggers in the future. Years after a car accident, the sound of screeching tires might trigger someone to respond with the same heightened fight-or-flight response they initially felt because the body is recalling that traumatic experience.

We know this about the human body, and yet releasing trauma from the body is a healing modality that is often overlooked. We most commonly see trauma and pain as problems of the mind and fail to acknowledge that the body is part of the healing process too. In his groundbreaking book *The Body Keeps the Score,* Bessel van der Kolk describes the impact of trauma stored in the body:

> Long after a traumatic experience is over, it may be reactivated at the slightest hint of danger and mobilize disturbed brain circuits and secrete massive amounts of stress hormones.... Traumatized people chronically feel unsafe inside their bodies: The past is alive in the form of gnawing interior discomfort. Their bodies are constantly bombarded by visceral warning signs, and, in an attempt to control these processes, they often become expert at ignoring their gut feelings and in numbing awareness of what is played out inside. They learn to hide from their selves.

While we all experience trauma, some people carry the record of it like an open emotional wound that has become a part of them, and others carry it like a journal entry in a notebook stored on a shelf. That is, some people hold the trauma so tightly that it becomes an identity, and others see it as one important thing—but not the only thing—that happened to them. Healing the body helps the brain shift from the former mindset to the latter.

When coupled with traditional therapy, body-based healing modalities can release layers of trauma stored in the body and unlock deeper healing. Each modality has its own approach, uses, and benefits, and each person needs something a little different because every body is energetically unique. By exploring the techniques that resonate with you, you can release pent-up energy and traumatic memories that may be keeping you stuck in emotional pain. (See the Resources section at the end of the book for a list of healing modalities you may wish to explore.)

We hang on to our traumas until we intentionally transform them. So one of the first steps in doing energy work is to determine where trauma is trapped in the body and understand the origin of the mental, emotional, and somatic wounds that hide there. In searching for these spots, it can feel like you are hunting for your most tender wounds so you can jab them. But when those uncomfortable sensations and emotions well up, that is a sign you are onto something, so keep going. If you can remain curious, discomfort and resistance will lead you to the pain that needs to be released. Signals might include sadness or fear, but avoidance, confusion, reluctance, and indecision are also indicators. Though these experiences and emotions might be uncomfortable, they help us ask the question: What is the origin point? Learning to get comfortable with discomfort is a practice that leads us to deeper healing.

The Energy of Emotion

As Dr. Hawkins teaches in *The Map of Consciousness Explained*, our emotions are energy in motion, or e-motion. The energy of emotions creates a sensation in our bodies—such as a tightened throat, sweaty palms, or a queasy stomach—that we interpret and label as an emotion. However, if we can move past the thinking mind and feel the energy moving through our body, then we can identify what we're feeling and choose how to respond to it instead of simply reacting based on past experiences. We can remain grounded, connected, and in control.

Because emotions are energy, they have different levels of vibration. Emotions that feel bad have low vibrations while emotions that feel good have higher vibrations.

The emotions at the low end of the vibrational spectrum cause us to feel depleted, numb, indifferent, listless, bored, humdrum, and passive. In more extreme cases, we might feel anger, rage, resentment, deep sadness, emptiness, or vengeance. Whether they show up as a total lack of energy or as an uncontrollable, frenzied amount of energy, low-vibrational emotions don't serve us in becoming the best version of ourselves.

On the other end of the spectrum, high-vibrational emotions cause us to feel excited, alive, passionate, purposeful, motivated, and action oriented. When our emotions start to climb in vibration, we can feel content, joyful, ecstatic, loving, accepting, blissful, peaceful, or even enlightened. These energies often give the feeling that we're in the right place at the right time, like everything is falling into place. High-vibrational emotions support us in becoming the best version of ourselves.

Ultimately, we tend to see poor self-image and decision-making when we're stuck in low-vibrational emotions, and we tend to see positive self-image and decision-making when we rise to high-vibrational emotions.

To shift an emotional state, you must feel the energy stored in the body without judging it. Then you can decide what it means and what to do about it. With practice, you can begin to choose your emotional states with intention and cultivate an inner world based on the support you need in the moment. You learn to feel the subtle and unique differences in each emotion, and this nuanced emotional intelligence allows you to access your agency and the healing process with more intention.

A Quick Tool: Sway Testing

While intentionally choosing our emotional state and trigger responses is crucial, it is rarely easy in practice. Since it requires us to stop and think before we let the emotion take control of mind and body, sway testing can help us find the pause.

Also known as muscle testing, sway testing is a simple method of tapping into the body's innate wisdom by asking it a question and seeing how it responds. Start with a grounding practice (see What Helped Me below); then while standing relaxed and balanced, ask yourself a yes/no question, such as "Is this food good for my body right now?" or "Will this action bring me peace?" Observe whether your body leans forward, indicating yes, or back, indicating no. The practice provides direct feedback from the body and its energy field. And because the body is attuned to truth, it is going to provide an honest answer. I find this method especially helpful in testing my intuition and choosing a course of action that feels aligned with my needs and values.

I know it might sound silly to think we can ask our body a question, but this is essentially the method David Hawkins used to develop the Map of Consciousness, conducting more than 250,000 calibrations over twenty years.

Healing from trauma—and energy work in particular—is an intensely personal process. So choose the modalities that resonate with you, and don't stop exploring until you find something that works—until you *feel* something that works. Let go of the "weird" and the uncomfortableness that comes with something new and "alternative" and give it a try. There are many restorative blessings to be found.

What Helped Me: Grounding Exercises

Energy work sometimes feels destabilizing. Though its purpose is to recalibrate your body back to its original state, it can still feel like the rug is being pulled out from underneath you. I have found it helps to start or end my energy practices with a grounding exercise. This technique can be especially helpful when your healing work brings up memories you would rather not relive. It keeps you grounded in the present moment, so you don't get pulled too far into the past.

There are many ways to ground or center your energy (visit my website, melissahull.com, or search online for "grounding techniques"). I will take you through one of my favorites: a simple body scan.

If possible, choose a location where you can plant your feet firmly on the earth. If you like the feeling of dirt or grass beneath your feet, go barefoot.

Take a few deep breaths, letting your feet and legs get heavier with each exhale.

Then, starting at the top of your head and working down, feel into your "energy field"—that is, feel the energy in and around your body. Wherever you find tension, pressure, or resistance, pause for a moment. Allow yourself to feel that sensation as much as you can tolerate, and with each deep breath, push the energy into the ground. For me, this process feels like I'm slowly moving the energy down through my body with each breath—and it can take time, especially as you build up your strength and practice.

Once you notice a sense of lightness and release, take a few deep breaths again. You might feel sturdier, taller, or something else entirely. Just notice it.

When you sense the grounding process is complete, hit the ground three times. This is a symbolic gesture that acknowledges the release and gives a sense of closure. If you prefer, you can clap, snap, or recite an affirmation—whatever feels right.

The body speaks; grounding and other tools simply help you listen.

CHAPTER TEN
NATURE

Dear Drew,
I can still hear the way you squealed with joy
while we spun in circles in the sunshine.
Love, Mom

EVEN WITH THE MOST intentional effort to heal, some days nothing seemed to help. When despondence took over, I sought solace in nature.

On a day when I felt particularly lost, I ventured to one of Drew's favorite spots. He loved all kinds of nature but felt most free at the beach, marveling at the trails of tiny footprints he left in the wet sand. When he first discovered their impermanence, he cried each time the surf washed them away. So I'd grab his hand, and we'd start running up the beach, leaving long lines of footprints beyond the waves' reach. Each time, he'd look up at me with fresh awe at the marks we left on the world.

As I sat on the beach, staring at the same stretch of sand where I once chased Drew, I listened to the rhythmic crashing of the waves and reflected on the vastness of this world and how connected I could still feel to it all. I was so small within it, yet there was endless room for me to expand. Rather than feeling terrified by how little control I had over the universe, I more easily appreciated its beauty. Amid the enormity of ocean and sky, I recognized the life force thrumming within me. I felt that irrefutable connection to something bigger, and my heart lifted.

On another of my spiritual treks, I headed to Flagstaff, anticipating serene greenery. Instead, I found swaths of scorched earth and woody skeletons. A wildfire had torn through the forest, and it was soot and ash as far as the eye could see. How could anything grow here? Walking deeper into the burned area, I crouched at the base of a blackened tree and pushed aside the ashy debris. With enough searching, I eventually unearthed new life sprouting beneath the charred leaves. As I touched the tender greenness emerging from the fire's path, I couldn't help but recognize my own potential for regrowth, renewal, and transformation. *Maybe I can grow bigger than my grief—even if I don't quite understand how yet.*

Since I couldn't escape to a perfectly picturesque destination every day, I sought other ways to nurture my connection with nature. A memory garden we created in Drew's honor—an intentionally designed space of remembrance open to all—became a cherished place for connecting with him and with nature. In the beginning, Devin and I would share a popsicle there, sometimes talking about Drew, sometimes not, but always feeling closer to him under the sunflowers he loved so much. Devin might bring a toy for Drew, or sometimes a little birdhouse. The garden was always there for us. Over the years, the people who loved Drew left mementos nestled like treasures throughout the garden—stones, angels, poems, plants, seeds. A sanctuary of little love letters, and I got to tend it.

CHAPTER 10: NATURE

Drew's garden quickly became my favorite space to practice healing. When I was indoors, I struggled to feel grounded, but in nature, I could easily assess my energy and manage my emotions. Nature was my touchpoint to consciousness. So I painted and journaled among the flowers. I walked until I accepted what I could not yet answer. I got my hands in the earth. Every day I showed up to the garden, nature came to my rescue. When I covered a seed with fresh earth or refilled the feeder for a baby hummingbird, the continuous cycles of nature reassured me. As I prepared the soil for another season of planting, pieces of me came back to life. Watching a butterfly land a bud away created enough stillness within me to notice I could still find peace inside my broken heart. Every time I set two feet—or two hands—on the dirt, life became a little more beautiful to me.

As I spent more time in nature, I felt connected to Drew in new ways. I no longer had to go to his grave to feel his presence; I felt it when I swung in his tire swing or leaned against the olive tree he used to climb. Nature's beauty helped bridge the past and present, bringing forward my memories of him in those places in a way that was no longer emotionally triggering.

Because I saw what happened to me when I was in nature, I trusted it. I knew that even when I didn't quite trust God, I could trust the universe.

WHEN GRIEF FEELS IMPOSSIBLY IMMENSE, NATURE HELPS US REDISCOVER A CONNECTION TO SOMETHING BIGGER.

Surrounded by ancient mountains or endless coastline, it becomes easier to sense a connection to something bigger than ourselves. The universe, life force, energy—whatever it is, you can *feel* it. Present in the vastness of nature, we can better understand our place within our experiences. When that type of introspection feels threatening, nature reconnects us to our inner world with calmness and ease. Noticing the life and beauty around us anchors us in the present, helping us find peace within our bodies and providing a space to hold our sorrow. By sitting in awe of the mountains, water, and trees, we allow our suffering to be held by the earth beneath us. When we immerse ourselves in nature, its wisdom can guide us through the complexities of loss, offering comfort and perspective when words or human presence fall short.

Scientific research supports this deeply felt experience. Studies show that spending time in natural settings can reduce stress hormones, lower blood pressure, and slow heart rates. These physiological changes shift us from a state of fight-or-flight into one of rest and restoration, creating space to process our emotions. A simple walk in nature can boost mood and enhance feelings of well-being, offering a gentle way to engage with grief without feeling overwhelmed.

Nature's cycles of growth and renewal remind us of our own profound capacity for transformation and healing. Life is resilient, designed to adapt and endure in the harshest environments. In nature, death and decay are not fearful or taboo—they are as essential to the cycle of life as birth itself. No matter how much damage has been done, we can still cultivate something beautiful and vibrant in its place. Ecotherapy, sometimes called nature therapy or green therapy, emphasizes this connection, highlighting how engaging with natural cycles fosters purpose and resilience, even amid profound challenges. In nature's reminders of resilience, we are invited to trust our own ability to grow in the face of pain.

CHAPTER 10: NATURE

When we can't yet see the beauty in life, cultivating it in nature can serve as a living symbol of connection, growth, and the enduring bond that transcends loss. Nurturing a piece of nature can become a sacred ritual—a way to channel the love and care we once gave a lost loved one. In the quiet act of caring for a plant or cultivating a garden, we create a space to pour our love and devotion, allowing it to grow into something new and meaningful. Research into horticultural therapy confirms that nurturing plants or creating gardens can significantly reduce feelings of grief, depression, and anxiety, while fostering a renewed sense of purpose and agency. These moments of care remind us that in loss, we can still nurture life and create something lasting.

For some people, stepping into nature might feel daunting. Grief can feel too heavy to carry outside, or the idea of solitude may seem overwhelming. It's all right to start small: sitting on the porch, opening a window to let the breeze in, or watching birds from a cafe. Even small interactions with nature—watching leaves sway or hearing birdsong—have been shown to enhance mental well-being and reduce feelings of loneliness. These "micro-restorative" moments still offer profound healing benefits. Nature is always there, waiting for us to engage with it, each in our own time and way.

By immersing in nature, we allow ourselves to heal not in isolation but in connection with the world around us. Nature's consistent renewal serves as a poignant reminder that while we have choice and agency in our healing, it still takes time. Like the seasons, we move through cycles of darkness and light. But the sun rises after every night, flowers bloom after the harshest winters, and just as the earth renews itself, so too will you.

What Helped Me: Nature Rituals

Engaging with nature can be a powerful way to support your grieving process. Here are several approaches I have found helpful in integrating nature into my healing journey. Try the ones that resonate with you, and adapt them as needed.

Meditative walk. During a regular time or in a regular place, go on a meditative walk. Move slowly and focus on your breath and surroundings, allowing pent-up emotions to release while the natural setting provides a soothing backdrop.

Memorial plant. Nurture a plant or design an intentional space in nature for healing or remembrance. Plant a tree, start a garden, or pot a single amaryllis on the windowsill so you can watch it put out elegant, trumpetlike blooms.

Gratitude token. Find a small natural object—a rock, shell, or feather—that resonates with you. Keep it with you as a reminder of a cherished memory or something you're grateful for. When overwhelmed, hold the object and reflect on its significance. This practice grounds you in positive memories, balancing grief with gratitude.

Nature observation. Visit the same spot in nature throughout the year, observing its changes with the seasons. Reflect on how your grief transforms over time as well. Let nature be a welcome mirror for your inner world.

In any of these nature practices, observe your inner state. See if you find more peace, more quiet in which you can hear the soft voice of your heart.

CHAPTER ELEVEN
CONNECTION

Dear Drew,
I've learned that it's okay to seek help
and lean on others during this time.
Love, Mom

AFTER DREW'S ACCIDENT, I had a lot of support from family. My siblings had an uncanny ability to sense when I needed them, often showing up at just the right moment with a listening ear or a comforting presence. Their strength gave me permission to feel my pain without judgment; their encouragement reminded me that I was still capable of finding my way forward. Whether through late-night phone calls, quiet moments spent together, or their constant reassurance that they were always there for me, they made it clear that I could lean on them whenever I needed.

I had one aunt who understood my pain without needing any explanation; she offered a kind of solace that didn't demand words or solutions. She didn't rush me or try to "fix" me; instead, she sat with me in stillness, validating my emotions and reminding me that it was fine to feel shattered. She never minimized my grief but instead reflected back to me the strength she saw, especially when I felt like I had none left. And she recounted her own stories of loss to remind me that my pain, while unique, was part of a shared human experience.

Perhaps my strongest advocate was my best friend. When a lot of other people disappeared, she still showed up. When Joey moved out and I was scared to go to sleep, I didn't even need to call her. She had already picked up the phone and invited me for a sleepover. "Just grab Devin and come over here." She was my rock—one of the few special people who could witness me in my deepest pain and withstand the devastation of it all. She held space for me well before I thought I deserved it, and she helped me put myself back together during a time when neither of us knew how. Most importantly, she never gave up trying to help, even when it required tender honesty.

Years after Drew's accident, we were out for dinner and my steak showed up incorrectly prepared, so I sent it back. After the server left, my best friend looked at me. "You know," she said, "sometimes you can be very snippy at restaurants." I was taken aback; I had only asked for my meal to be prepared as ordered. She continued, "You come across as intimidating sometimes. Not around me, but more than once I've had to defend you when you weren't around. Why do you think you show up that way?"

I knew I was formidable when I was angry—I could feel the force surging through me—but on a day-to-day basis, I thought I was friendly and approachable. Wow, was my perception off. Apparently, my heavy emotions seeped into my demeanor, causing me to show up to others as fearsome. Devin reinforced that perception. "Oh, yeah, Mom. One of the classroom moms thinks you don't like her. And the other one wants you to volunteer, but she is too scared to ask you."

Holy cow. I still had a lot of healing work to do. And it was a good thing I had my best friend there to help me. I needed as much support as I could get.

Building connections with supportive people means we don't have to do our healing work alone.

In many ways, grief brings clarity, sort of like looking through binoculars. When you hold them up to your eyes, at first everything is blurry; then you turn the dial, and suddenly everything comes into focus. Filtered through the lens of loss, everything about life becomes bigger and clearer. When we have been changed so fundamentally, our relationships are affected as well. And whether we want to or not, we may gain new clarity about those relationships. Sometimes they become a source of strength, and other times they become difficult to navigate or heartbreaking when things go wrong. If we have clear expectations, we can navigate inevitable hiccups and recognize true connection and friendship when they show up.

In my journey, I have identified four types of people: those who are *with* you, those who are *for* you, those who are *neither* with you nor for you, and those who are both with you *and* for you. It's important to know the difference.

With-you people. There are many people who are *with* you but not genuinely *for* you. These are the people who show up as long as it works for them, or as long as they're getting something by doing so, but you wouldn't call them when you're truly in need. Some will say, "I want to see you get better," but then turn around and actively throw debris in your path, booby-trapping your progress. I had one group of friends from a social organization who showed up after Drew's accident—bringing me casseroles and setting up coffee dates. But after an initial flush of activity, they never checked in, and then I found out several had broken my confidence and gossiped about me. I chose to let them go because they didn't have my best interests in mind. Unfortunately, this is more common than we want it to be. Pay attention to what people do, not merely to what they say.

For-you people. There are also many people who are genuinely *for* you, but they're not actually *with* you. Therapists, clergy, and other support folks can fall into this group; they legitimately assist you in healing, but they can't be there 24/7. And some of the people with whom we have these kinds of relationships are supportive but stop showing up when grief makes things messy. They don't know what to say, so they fall silent. They're not sure how to help, so they grow distant. They might send a text to let you know they're thinking of you—because they do care—but it generally stops there. (I do have empathy for the folks who don't know what to say when someone is grieving, because, truly, it is difficult, awkward, and uncomfortable. If you think you might fall into this category for someone, I'll encourage you to make an effort even if you feel uncomfortable. Remember, the person grieving has already lost a loved one and lost normalcy in their life—isolation doesn't help.)

Not-with-you-or-for-you people. When people stop showing up at all—not offering *any* kind of love or support—they are not-with-you-or-for-you people. But that's a mouthful, so I like to think of them as "rip-cord relationships." The minute things get tough, they rip the cord, and they're out. These people are the ones making last-minute cancellations and excuses for their absence in your life. While of course plans must change occasionally, consistent absence tells you what you need to know. In the worst case, not-with-you-or-for-you folks are bad actors, which I'll come back to in a moment.

With-you-for-you people. With-you-for-you people show up when you need them. They don't merely make a verbal commitment; they are a physical presence. "What do you need? I can be there in twenty minutes." But they do more than show up. They have your back even when you are not around. They see you, and they help you see yourself. They love you in your weak moments, and they celebrate when you get things right. A with-you-for-you relationship is one of those rare safe spaces where you can just *be*, even when that means messing up or falling apart or both.

With-you-for-you people love you through the learning process. They don't pull away; they lean in. When you lean back, they don't use your weak moments as fodder for gossip. They respect your vulnerability and keep it private. A true with-you-for-you friend sits with you in pain and reminds you that you are stronger for surviving it. Sometimes with-you-for-you support means uncomfortable honesty, as it did when my best friend confronted me about my intimidating behavior. From love, with-you-for-you friends ask hard questions, and they are by your side for as long as it takes to arrive at the answers. We need people who aren't afraid to tell us when they see trouble; we might disagree with their observations, but mutual respect means the relationship is not at stake. When we lose our way, these are the people who remember the best of us while we find our way back.

With-you-for-you people are my people.

• • •

After Drew's accident, I initially assumed that anyone who showed up had good intentions, but I quickly learned I could trust some people and not others. Beyond the gossips, I was shocked to find truly bad actors, people who used our family's tragedy to take advantage of us. Without going into undue detail, I'll say we trusted a colleague and friend to assist us with financial matters, and that person did not act with integrity. Our grief was not a deterrent; it was used as an opportunity.

My caution to you: Even when you feel incapacitated by grief, be careful not to surrender your agency so much that you make yourself vulnerable to more injury. Financial and legal matters in particular must be attended to. Alert your bank of your situation so that if you forget to pay a bill or an unusual transaction appears, they know to flag it and offer you assistance. Likewise, contact any other critical accounts to make sure nothing is overlooked or that you get a grace period while dealing with more pressing matters. If you give anyone access to your accounts, make absolutely sure they are with-you-for-you people or that they are professionals with a fiduciary duty to act in your best interest.

Your vulnerability should never be an opportunity for someone to cause further harm. Even in grief, you must advocate for yourself.

• • •

By cultivating an awareness of our relationships, we can make a conscious choice about the depth of relationship we want with each person. We can identify what each relationship provides and doesn't provide, and then adjust our expectations or boundaries accordingly. Or we can choose to say goodbye.

And let me be clear: People with whom we have the first three types of relationships can still be lovely people to spend time with, and sometimes that is enough. Our with-you friends show up when we need surface-level distraction or fun, but they can't be trusted with our vulnerability. Our for-you friends know how to support us when they're available, but they can't be relied on. Rip-cord relationships might be enjoyable while they last, but they can't be trusted or relied on. Most of us can probably count our with-you-for-you people on one hand. But once we get good at recognizing them, it becomes easier to add more to our life.

I want to assure you that it is acceptable to recognize these differences, and in some cases, it is imperative. When we let people go, like pruning a rosebush, it makes room for healthier things to grow. We must be willing to accept that not every friendship is lifelong; it might last one beautiful season, meaningful for the particular phase of growth we are in. As we blossom, so should our friendships. If they can't, they were meant for a single season. We can find gratitude in that.

Loss lets us view our relationships with more honesty. As a result, we also see ourselves in a more compassionate way as we choose the best relationships for us.

WHAT HELPED ME: RELATIONSHIP REFLECTION

When our relationships are tested by grief, clarity and compassion can be our most valuable tools. I suggest setting aside some time to reflect on what your relationships mean to you. How do you feel about the different types of relationships in your life? How has grief affected or changed them, if at all?

If relationships are particularly complicated for you, or if you're curious to dig deeper, try conducting a relationship inventory. Make a list of the people you interact with regularly or who you consider significant in your life.

- Can you recognize your with-you-for-you people?
- Who's *for* you but not actually *with* you?
- Who's *with* you but maybe not entirely *for* you?
- Are you comfortable with those relationships staying the way they are? Or do some of them need to change? Do they require some loving conversations—or a goodbye?

Try not to judge your answers as they come up. When we can see and accept people for who they are, we can make more thoughtful decisions about our relationships—and feel more connection than disconnection in trying times.

PART THREE

Face the Tough Stuff

FACING THE TOUGHEST TRUTHS of grief and healing is like reaching into a bowl full of fishhooks. Each hook reveals something sharp and painful, and as you tug one, you discover a messy tangle of buried narratives, locked-up emotions, and wounds—each linked to another and leading you back to places you thought you'd long since left behind.

You know this work will hurt. But awareness, painful as it might be, gives you power: the power to choose, the power to see clearly the stories you've been telling yourself and to decide which ones to disentangle. Healing is frustrating and overwhelming, and it demands willingness and courage. Each time you reach in to unhook a single barb, you cannot know how many others will come with it. Pricked and tender, you must own your part in the pain, wade through the discomfort, and confront the truths you've hidden from yourself.

I will not ask you to labor alone—and I would never urge you to risk the barbs unless I had endured them first. I promise to remind you how transformative this work is each time you reach into the bowl. Healing is not easy, but it is yours to claim. So when you're ready, reach in. One hook at a time. One choice at a time.

Keep going.

CHAPTER TWELVE
AWARENESS

Dear Drew,
I am learning to be gentle with myself as I heal.
Love, Mom

IN THE EARLY DAYS of motherhood, I struggled with the noise and messiness of children. I could not tolerate my kids leaving their toys all over the house. Loud play had to be taken outside. Sticky handprints, rambunctious make-believe, and even squeals of joy were enough to send me over the edge. Noise and mess had always bothered me—blaring TVs and booming voices made me jumpy, and I liked everything in its place. With children, of course, I could never get away from either noise or mess. But when I found myself spanking Drew because—yet again—he hadn't cleaned up his Tonka trucks, I knew it was time to check myself. Where was my reactiveness coming from?

I chose to work with a parenting coach to learn some strategies that would help me navigate tough moments. I started by building an awareness of the sensations that would arise in my body during those stressful episodes with my kids. When the chaos got to me—sometimes to the point I shook—rather than focusing on the boys, I would head out to the backyard and stand with both feet planted firmly on the ground. As the sun beat down on my skin, the cool earth calmed me from the soles up. Taking a deep breath of fresh air, I would pause. Gradually full breaths would return, jagged at first and then more rhythmic as I let the breeze carry away my anxiety.

Simple techniques like this one helped me manage my reactions, respond with more intention, and create positive behavioral change for both me and the boys. I am so grateful I sought this help when I did. It made a big difference in how I interacted with Drew and Devin, bringing me closer to both and making my last days with Drew richer and more rewarding.

Years later, as Drew's loss drove me deeper into energy work and other healing practices, I gained more insight into my struggle with mess and noise. I started to see how my past experiences and my healing were connected. When I was about ten, my mother received a diagnosis of terminal cancer, which she battled through most of my childhood and early adulthood. (She lived for more than twenty years after her first diagnosis. Each time she got a new diagnosis, we were told she was going to die, so, in a way, we were ready for her death—unlike Drew's.) During her treatments, my mom stayed with her parents, so for a few years we saw her only periodically. When she was home, our lives revolved around her rest, and waking her brought consequences. We four kids could play, but we had to do so quietly or go outside. My dad worked long hours in the hot Arizona sun to make sure we had enough money to pay for my mom's treatments. By the time he came home, he did not have the time or energy to pick up after us, so that responsibility fell on our shoulders, especially mine as the oldest child. A forgotten toy or burst of

CHAPTER 12: AWARENESS

laughter often meant I was the one disciplined, which sometimes meant corporal punishment.

While the parenting techniques I learned from my coach improved my parenting when my boys were young, I never fully understood what churned inside me: Why would my body shake when they got too loud? Once I started searching out the origins of my triggers and mapping their connections, everything clicked. My shaking wasn't random; it was rooted in my childhood. Of course I feared a noisy, messy home. Growing up, I had no space to be a child. I had to stay controlled, quiet, neat, and focused on everyone else's needs instead of my own. It took me years to see it, but every dash to the backyard had been an instinctive attempt to ground myself—reconnecting to the wisdom of my body so I could address the noise in my mind. By feeling my feet rooted to the ground, I was bringing the scared little girl self out of our childhood home and into the present moment where I could reassure her that she was safe. Only then could I give my boys a childhood experience different from mine.

With that realization, many others flooded in. I had lived my whole life believing my aversion to noise and mess was merely a personality trait. In actuality, it was a trauma response, triggered and amplified by the chaos of raising kids. My anxiety was not about my own children; it was about a child who didn't understand why she was in trouble all the time. I had internalized my childhood directives so completely that I ended up creating the same rigid set of rules for my boys that I had spent a lifetime resenting.

Once I saw the issue, I couldn't unsee it. If I didn't address my wounds, I risked becoming the one to perpetuate this damaging cycle. By the time I realized this, spanking was no longer an issue, but my stringent need for order still limited the creative freedom that should underscore childhood. Determined to break free from these patterns, I kept working on myself—this time supported by the tools I had discovered while grieving. With a deeper understanding of my past, I made significant progress.

I want to be clear that even though I knew this was the most important work of my life, these tough realizations about my parenting did not feel like a win; I felt embarrassed and defeated. The win was that I chose to be brave enough and vulnerable enough to work on my childhood wounds. As I faced a part of myself I was not proud of, I saw my strength gradually emerge. Although learning the origin of my struggles humbled me, the results changed me for the better—and that was well worth facing the memory of painful reprimands.

To heal the whole person, no part can be left behind.

Facing past wounds demands courage most of us fear we don't have. Instead of revisiting the origin of our pain to reprocess it at the root, we cling to the familiar ache of trauma because it feels easier and safer. We let anger win and say to hell with the consequences; we give in to sadness and lose another day under the covers; we submit to shame as we allow negative self-talk to ring like truth.

But the thought of dealing with unprocessed trauma is much scarier than actually doing it. Choosing to reopen a wound is hard, but once you have made that decision, I promise the work is not as terrifying or damning or pointless as your fears tell you. Healing requires us to expose our most tender, aching wounds, and then it puts those wounds in the spotlight. While that feels deeply unsettling at first, it brings enormous benefits. When we choose to learn from the past, we are rewarded with a new perspective and the ability to see a better future. By unpacking my past in a safe and supportive setting, I could acknowledge the connection between my parenting struggles and past trauma. Then, I could view my mistakes with more compassion and less judgment, accept them, and start healing—without shame and self-criticism sabotaging my efforts.

Figure 2 shows how I envision the path from childhood trauma through awareness to find emotional healing. As you'll see, it involves identifying and changing our behavior patterns, often with the help of therapy. While the figure appears to show a nice, neat linear process, don't forget that healing does not travel a straight path. Nonetheless, it helps to understand how the elements connect.

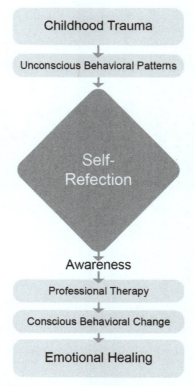

Figure 2. The path from trauma through awareness to healing.

However, we must look at the past with an honest assessment and an understanding of our motivations. Anger in particular is commonly faced when viewing the past, as repressed hurt often surfaces as anger. Some people label anger as "negative," but emotions themselves are neither negative nor positive; how they are used is the issue. In fact, I take a strong position that anger can have positive effects when channeled properly. At its best, anger allows us to identify our boundaries in a way that spurs us to action—because we feel a great offense, we can no longer stay silent; because we have been violated, we seek self-preservation. At its worst, anger is used to cause reciprocal harm—someone hurt us, so we use our anger to hurt them back. But two wrongs don't make a right, and in the healing process, the goal is not to get even but rather to elevate. Sometimes we don't see our motivations, behaviors, and choices with as much clarity as we'd like. Other times, we may see our choices but not understand what is driving them. By sitting with a traumatic memory long enough, with the right intention, we open ourselves to a new level of awareness and deeper healing. Experiences we are not consciously thinking about may come forward to show us old pain in fresh light. And we can do better because we know better.

When I first attempted this deeper level of healing, I thought all my pain stemmed from Drew's death. I carried an enormous wound, and that was the obvious place to start. But I discovered I needed to address a lifetime of hurt that began long before Drew's accident. The busyness of everyday life masked a multitude of wounds. Periodically, I would erupt, those buried traumas bubbling up in the form of marital problems or work drama. Drew's loss heightened all these issues, but they originated in deeper layers. I had to dig

CHAPTER 12: AWARENESS

through all the crap I had buried; I had to look at the parts of my life—the parts of *me*—that did not serve my highest and best self. And, honestly, if I could have kept all that crap hidden and buried, maybe I would have. But I had tried that approach already, and it didn't give me the life I wanted.

The more we can courageously see ourselves—past and present—the more agency we possess to choose what we want in the future. In fact, it is when we reject and deny parts of ourselves that we lose the ability to change our trajectory. We end up continually visiting trauma loops that keep us in a cycle of avoidance, self-loathing, and missed growth opportunities. If we are not willing to take an honest look at certain parts of ourselves, then we are not likely to accept them or find the clarity we need to transform them.

Everyone has their own ugly stuff. We can't change that. But our relationship with the ugly stuff can change. We can prepare ourselves before going into potentially triggering situations so that we navigate them more skillfully. We can quiet our internal and external reactions by becoming aware of where the original trauma occurred—and reminding ourselves that we are no longer trapped in that moment. When we can engage in our lives with less fear and confusion, we have the ability to be more present. And though we do need to revisit the past, healing begins in the now. Our thoughts often drift between regret over the past and anxiety about the future, trapping us in a cycle of mental and emotional unrest. Present-moment awareness liberates us from this cycle, allowing us to experience life as it unfolds.

Being present is an act of conscious observation. When we tune in to our thoughts, feelings, and bodily sensations without judgment, we uncover patterns and triggers that influence our behavior. When we notice recurring thoughts like *I can't believe I made that mistake last week* they are accompanied by feelings of guilt and physical sensations such as tightness in the chest. By acknowledging these experiences with curiosity rather than criticism, we can reframe our inner dialogue: *This guilt is teaching me something valuable. I can grow from this moment rather than dwell on the past.* (Do you see how this links to our earlier discussion of energy work?)

Mindfulness practices such as meditation, breathwork, and journaling are powerful tools for cultivating this present-moment awareness. These practices teach us to let go of judgment, creating space for self-compassion and healing. As we anchor ourselves in the now, we learn to release the grip of past wounds and future fears, opening the door to greater peace and self-acceptance.

Awareness deepens when we turn inward to examine the complex interplay of our thoughts, emotions, and actions. By identifying and understanding our emotional states and recognizing their origins, we can learn to respond to them in constructive ways. We can develop the skill to regulate emotions rather than be ruled by them. If you perceive neglect, you might think, *They never prioritize my needs*, and feel a surge of resentment along with a racing heartbeat and clenched fists. Without awareness, this reaction could lead to a heated argument or emotional withdrawal. However, with awareness, you can pause and reflect: *I feel hurt because I value being seen and heard. Instead of reacting impulsively, I can express my feelings calmly.*

This pause is a moment of transformation that allows us to feel and understand our emotions rather than suppress them or project them outward. Over time, such practices create emotional resilience. We learn to observe our inner storms without being swept away, making room for healing to occur. Tools like journaling and therapy can aid in this process, offering a safe space to explore emotions and gain clarity about their roots. As self-awareness grows, we become more adept at regulating our emotions, fostering a sense of inner stability that supports our healing journey.

The journey of awareness is a continuous process of learning, unlearning, and relearning. There will be moments of discomfort as you confront your patterns and recognize your role in perpetuating pain. Yet it is through this discomfort that growth occurs. Awareness is both the mirror that reflects our truth and the light that guides us forward. Each moment of mindfulness, each act of self-reflection, brings us closer to the life we desire—one of authenticity, peace, and profound healing. In becoming more aware, we do not just heal ourselves; we contribute to a world where understanding and compassion can flourish.

What Helped Me: Awareness Exercises

Because exploring past wounds can feel threatening, I suggest starting on the page—a safe, private space where you can let feelings come up without getting anyone else involved. This type of reflection is easier when you aren't triggered or destabilized, so choose a time when you feel prepared, supported, and ready to do some deep work. Before you begin, get centered by taking a few deep breaths, saying a prayer, or doing a body scan. Then do some reflective writing. I like to use prompts for this type of work, so here are two exercises that have brought me many insights.

Timeline. To trace the origins of triggers and uncover connections between past and present, draw a timeline of your life. Mark significant events on it, focusing on moments tied to emotions like fear, anger, or sadness. Look for recurring themes (for example, being criticized for noise or punished for mess) and any connections to your current challenges; circle the events that feel most impactful. Consider how these moments shaped your beliefs and behaviors. What insights can you apply to your present life?

Tetherball. To identify limiting beliefs, think about a game of tetherball. Imagine you are the ball, hanging out on the pole, enjoying your afternoon on the playground. Then someone walks up and hits you hard. The force of it takes you around and around the pole until you run out of rope. You realize that even on your best day you'll never get beyond the length of that rope. Quickly answer:
- What does this rope represent (for instance, a belief, a fear, or a pattern)?
- What are you being pulled back to?
- Who or what controls the force hitting you?
- Visualize cutting the rope and soaring freely. Where would you go? What would it feel like?

To heal the person we are today, we must look back at the versions of us that still carry wounds, and we need to let them be heard. These exercises help show us where our wounds hide.

CHAPTER THIRTEEN
GRACE

Dear Drew,
Some days are harder than others,
and I allow myself to feel whatever comes up.
Love, Mom

SHORTLY AFTER DREW'S FUNERAL, Joey thought we should take the family to Disneyland to lift Devin's spirits and give us one good day. To me, it felt wrong to go without Drew, but I acquiesced because I thought it was the best choice for our family.

As soon as we got there, I knew I had made a mistake. It was too soon. Everything about Disneyland broke my heart: the Peter Pan ride, the ice cream stand, the Simba character. Every attraction Drew once loved felt like a dagger in my heart. I had barely laid him to rest, and walking through "the happiest place on Earth" made it feel like we had moved on with our lives. So I was already on emotionally shaky ground when we got to Tarzan's Treehouse.

I climbed up the tree with Devin, the song "You'll Be in My Heart" by Phil Collins playing in the background. Drew loved that song. As I listened to lyrics about a bond that could not be broken, I could not maintain my composure anymore. A few steps from the bottom of the treehouse, I crumbled. Trembling, heaving, gasping for air, I grieved for my son in the middle of Disneyland.

As my crying became more violent, people started looking at me, wondering what was wrong. When someone asked if I was all right, the only thing I could get out was "I just lost my son." And as soon as the words left my mouth, a man, a total stranger, wrapped his arms around me and started slowly helping me down. I will never forget the look of sheer compassion on his face—it is etched into my mind. As I wailed and shook in his arms, his kindness never faltered. He didn't look away. He didn't apologize for me. He simply sat there, witnessing my deepest pain.

Once again, I found myself clinging to the kindness of a stranger —a woman who writes me a letter, a man in a tree. These perfect strangers gave me what I needed most—hope, compassion, grace— when I was desperate for someone to see how hard I was fighting. Without knowing anything else about me, this man knew I deserved grace. He treated me in a way I couldn't yet treat myself. As the rattling of my breath steadied, I heard my heart whisper, *If a total stranger can show you that kind of compassion, then can't you?*

Although it would take me many years to fully integrate the concept of grace into my life, a simple form of it held me steady when the waves of grief threatened to pull me under. It found me in quiet moments—the morning sun filtering through the kitchen window and casting a golden glow on the empty chair where Drew used to sit; his favorite teddy bear that I would hug, feeling its worn fur beneath my fingers. When guilt and regret came crashing in, grace offered forgiveness. Sitting by Drew's favorite tree in the garden, a silent testament to life continuing despite loss, I learned to forgive myself for the what-ifs and if-onlys, letting go of the weight that threatened to drown me.

A few years later, friends and family suggested going to Disneyland to celebrate Drew's birthday. I felt conflicted; I still didn't know if I could emotionally handle it. Instead, I ended up visiting Drew's gravesite, as had become my tradition on his birthday. But I remember setting flowers next to his grave and thinking, *Maybe we should have gone to Disneyland. Maybe it's okay to do things he would have loved rather than coming here and feeling sad.* That was the last year I needed to spend his birthday at the cemetery.

The following year, we returned to Disneyland, and I went back up in the Tarzan Tree. I climbed the steps as kids ran around me, wearing their Tarzan costumes and laughing in excitement. The Phil Collins song still played in the background, but this time I knew Drew was in my heart and we were doing this together, forever. And that's how I have felt ever since.

> **WE DESERVE TO SHOW OURSELVES THE SAME GRACE, COMPASSION, AND FORGIVENESS WE RECEIVE FROM OTHERS.**

The word *grace* has many definitions, encompassing qualities from elegance to kindness to unconditional love. We witness its expression in a dancer's quiet strength, a stranger's warm smile, and a parent's unwavering patience. In a religious context, grace is the gift of divine love without the onus of earning it. This is closest to the meaning I am using in this chapter. When we show ourselves grace, we offer ourselves love and kindness, even when we're not sure we deserve it. We welcome our imperfections, reframe our supposed failures, and embrace our humanity without judgment. Grace helps us see the truth of a situation without blame.

Showing kindness to others often feels natural. When we see someone hurting, friend or stranger, we feel pulled to them. We see their humanness. But when it comes to ourselves, our critical inner voice insists we don't deserve the same care. The comfort of the pain we know outweighs the discomfort of the self-compassion we're not yet accustomed to receiving, and punishment feels more natural than self-compassion. It's like we've misplaced the instruction manual for showing ourselves kindness.

When a perfect stranger showed me the compassion I couldn't yet extend to myself, it interrupted my pattern of self-hate and self-blame long enough to let the light shine in. For a moment, I could see that as much as others might blame me, no one was hurting me more than I was. I glimpsed what I needed to begin reframing my understanding of grace, compassion, and forgiveness—though it would take me years to fully do so.

At first, it was incredibly hard to show myself grace. How could I think anything but *You know you're a bad mom—you shouldn't have fallen asleep?* But a gentler, more compassionate voice began to emerge: *You were managing two little boys on your own, and you'd gotten four hours of sleep over three days. You were exhausted and needed help.*

As I listened to this kinder perspective, I began to see the larger picture. Even in my fatigue, I was still operating with my heart's truest intention, which was to keep my boys safe and to be a good mom. The harsh voice argued, *If you hadn't fallen asleep, this wouldn't have happened.* But the gentler voice countered, *That's not necessarily true.*

He could have slipped out when you were busy cooking in the kitchen or when someone else was watching him while you ran to the store.

The fact is, we make choices every day, and most of the time we don't notice where they lead unless something goes wrong. My choice to go check on Devin didn't cause Drew to fall into a canal, just as asking a spouse to stop at the drycleaner on the way home from work doesn't cause them to get in a car crash. Life does not always follow a simple equation of cause and effect. Not everything has an answer. Not everything can be known, prevented, or controlled, and not every bad outcome needs blame assigned. Sometimes things happen. Grace allows us to see that truth. I was responsible for providing a safe environment for my children, and grace helped me see that's what I was striving to do. When I offered myself grace, I saw the possibility of a life beyond shame and blame.

Grace also opens the door to compassion—for ourselves and for others. When we show ourselves kindness, we cultivate a deeper empathy and understanding of the human condition. We become less judgmental and more curious. We learn to see beyond the pain to the lessons and insights it offers. We will talk about empathy more in Chapter 17.

At its heart, grace embraces forgiveness, which is the closest thing I have found to real-life magic—it creates an opening that allows in all of the good and none of the bad. Perhaps the most magical outcome forgiveness creates is emotional freedom. When you truly forgive yourself and others, you are no longer tethered to the causal experience or the pain it brought you. Forgiveness does not change what happened, but it can change your relationship with that event. And in my experience, it is the only way to release the pain from your heart, so you can make space for something beautiful.

Inspiring a chain of positive emotions, grace ignites our healing process in the best way, but it takes practice to recognize and enact. And if we wait passively, grace may never appear. Sometimes we resist forgiveness because we fear it may diminish the wrongdoing or hurt caused by us or others. Maybe we fear that the hurt is our punishment to endure. But forgiveness is not about forgetting or excusing past traumas. It is about acknowledging them and choosing to see the opportunity for growth that remains.

The tricky part is that as soon as you show yourself the compassion or forgiveness you deserve, your critical voice immediately says, *You're letting yourself off the hook—big mistake.* When extending grace to yourself feels impossible, try flipping the script on your critical voice. Ask yourself: If someone I loved was in my position, would I judge them this harshly? Put anyone else in your place—a sibling, parent, or friend—and ask yourself if you would punish them forever. When I did this, I even asked: If Drew had been the dad who fell asleep that day, would I deny him grace? Would I want him to deny himself grace? I never found a yes with that line of questioning. As soon as I put someone I loved "on trial," I could not possibly sentence them to the same mental and emotional prison I had locked myself in. I had to stop believing I was the single irredeemable person in the story. If everyone else deserved forgiveness, then why didn't I?

When we see grace as a choice, it becomes an active process, something we can participate in and guide. We can build it over time, through intentional practice, instead of waiting to stumble across it. We deepen it with each and every act of kindness we extend to ourselves. Grace grows as we grow, becoming a powerful force for resilience, compassion, and healing.

What Helped Me: Childhood Photo

When I was working on self-forgiveness, one tool helped me break through my mental barriers and resistance more than any other: a childhood photo of myself. In the photo, I'm in kindergarten, wearing my favorite tulip dress with the blue collar, my hair pulled back. When I looked at that photo, I witnessed happiness and innocence.

As an adult, I felt the need to always take accountability and to be "perfect." If I was not perfect, someone would have something to say—that's what I was used to. But I had different expectations for the child in the photo than I had for the adult in the mirror. Any time I felt tempted to beat myself up or deny myself a kindness, I pulled out the photo. Seeing myself as a child, I could more easily acknowledge what I deserved then and what I deserved now. I could say, "I'm not going to scold you. I'm not going to tell you to shut up. I will never throw you in the corner and leave you to deal with your feelings alone. I'm going to sit here with you because I love you and I want us to be better."

Carrying around a childhood photo may seem like a simple tool, but it holds the power to unlock insights you might miss without the visual reminder that you deserve unconditional love—even from yourself.

CHAPTER FOURTEEN
OWNERSHIP

Dear Drew,
I find strength in the memories
that are etched in my heart.
Love, Mom

IN THE MIDST OF MOURNING DREW, I was blindsided by the revelation that my husband had been unfaithful—an additional wound to an already-fragile heart. My initial reaction was anger, deep and consuming. It felt fierce and justified, serving as a barrier against more pain. I let my frustration fly like a sword, cutting through anyone who wronged me—and the offense didn't have to be much for me to wield it. If a mom looked at me the wrong way in line for pickup, I'd confront her. If another kid gave Devin a hard time about his home life, I did not mince words with their parents. When I walked into school, people cleared a path.

Part of me welcomed my negative emotions because I could use them as permission slips, reacting to people and circumstances as the most wounded version of me—and she was *fierce*. But I mistook her "no one can touch me, everyone will pay" attitude as a source of inner power.

One day, I had a bone to pick with Devin's teacher about how she had handled something in the classroom, so I stomped through the school to find her. Quickly, I initiated an intense exchange about Devin's needs. I could tell she wanted to keep her cool, but I was determined to escalate the argument.

As I got ready to launch into an impassioned, blame-ridden monologue, something shifted. Suddenly, I could see and hear myself from someone else's perspective.

And I was horrified.

I stopped in the middle of my sentence and paused long enough to hear the voice of my heart: *You're messing this up.* This time, I listened.

"You know, I have to apologize," I said, surprising myself.

She stared at me, stunned and confused.

I continued, "I am not being fair, and I'm so sorry. I don't know why I'm approaching this conversation this way, because I wanted your cooperation, and right now I'm being anyone but the kind of person you'd want to cooperate with. So let me stop and take responsibility for what I just did. I'm being a jerk."

She looked at me for another moment before replying, "Thank God you said that, because I almost grabbed my handbag and walloped you upside the head."

"Well, I wouldn't blame you."

We held each other's gaze for another breath and then burst into laughter.

CHAPTER 14: OWNERSHIP

After defusing the tension I had created, I walked away with a stronger relationship with Devin's teacher and a solution we both could accept. But for the rest of the day, I couldn't stop thinking about how I had walked into that classroom full of anger over a completely solvable problem.

That day, I saw myself clearly for the first time in years.

Almost overnight, what had initially felt powerful suddenly felt shameful and lonely. When you enter a room, you want people to gravitate toward you, especially when you're in pain. Imagine how torturous it is when they avoid you instead. I had been so afraid of getting hurt by people and circumstances that were outside my control that I had become the one doing the hurting. When I finally woke up to the realization, I was too alone to be hurt by anyone anymore. My fear of an outcome had caused my most feared outcome.

I didn't do anything to deserve the things that had happened to me, but what I chose to do about them would make or break the rest of my life. I decided I loved myself more than I hated everyone else.

Over the next weeks and months, I worked my tools through the new lens of ownership. In the areas of life where I felt stuck, what could I take responsibility for? What choices did I have, and which ones would help me create change in the right direction? Where was I surrendering my power or confusing it with force? Where was I choosing to stay in a negative cycle with toxic beliefs and disempowering mindsets? Enormous clarity came from this time of reflection once I opened up the honest, compassionate voice of my heart. Taking ownership of my emotions and how I behaved allowed me to move forward.

TO HEAL FROM OUR PAIN, WE MUST OWN OUR CONTRIBUTIONS TO IT.

Though it is crucial to acknowledge how we contribute to our pain if we want to heal from it, I want to start this conversation by saying I fully understand that there are some situations in which we truly are victims of another person or circumstance—situations to which we have *no* contribution. We do not contribute to our own abuse, oppression, or victimization. Those are another person's choices enacted on us, and sometimes we have no power to stop them. I have lived through several such experiences, and that's exactly why I focus so much of my time and energy on the sense of empowerment that can be found in the aftermath of trauma.

We did not choose our pain and loss—I want to be *so, so clear* on that—but we do get to choose how that experience changes us. What happens after our toughest moments is our choice and our responsibility. That choice must be made with clarity, ownership, and agency. If we never ask ourselves what we can be accountable for, then we may never try to change our situation. If we do not acknowledge that we have some agency and the ability to use it, then we will never find our way out of the dark, desolate place where trauma left us.

This work is not easy. It is where we face the tough stuff and finally defeat our fiercest demons. We must own everything that comes from our most painful experiences, no matter how ugly or unfair, so that we can figure out what to do with it. We are all touched by trauma in some way, but if we focus only on the part of trauma we can't control—the thing that happened to us—then we surrender our agency to heal from it.

The Surprising Benefits of Emotional Swampland

Sometimes when I talk about this angry period of my life, I describe it as the time I was a prickly cactus living in stinky swampland. My barbs were sharp weapons that pricked others before they could prick me. Marked by the stench of unresolved pain, I had grown nose blind to my own odor. I had ventured deep into emotionally unsteady territory, sinking in the muck of my own delusions, until I finally stopped to realize I'd built my permanent residence there.

For a time, we all find ourselves being cactuses in an emotional swampland. It can even be necessary to stay there while we feel those prickly, mucky feelings. This phase of healing gives our most difficult and shameful feelings space to air out. Swampland has a purpose—as long as you don't get stuck there—and offers some surprising benefits.

Clarity. Throughout my entire healing process, I have found it helps to figure out a positive lesson from each challenge, so I gain a sense of "leveling up." Sometimes I find a lot to learn or obvious wisdom to hold onto. But during this period of my life, I didn't want any of it. I only knew that I wanted to get out of my emotional swampland. That's where I found clarity: I would no longer accept deception or toxicity in my relationships. That clarity was a gift. So I took the gift and the grueling work that came with it. I pulled my feet out of the muck and trucked myself outta there. I didn't have it all figured out, but I knew I needed to leave.

Take the clarity, take the gift, and move forward.

Accountability. When events or relationships don't turn out the way we want, we can be reluctant to take responsibility for our contributions to the outcome. I did not want to be accountable for Joey's cheating, and I wasn't—I didn't choose Joey's actions. However, I did have an intuition about my marriage that I kept ignoring, a gut feeling I kept shutting down. By tuning out what I didn't want to hear from my inner voice, I prolonged my own suffering. I had accepted a form of self-abandonment that I would never allow again.

When you take accountability for your choices, you own the good ones, the bad ones, the ones you regret, and the ones that result in unintended consequences. You are allowed to make a wrong choice (many, in fact), but let yourself learn and grow from it. And don't let your fear stop you from acknowledging that it *was* a choice.

Self-determination. I am a largely trusting person; I see the best in others and believe they are mostly good. I wanted to continue believing that, but I would need to do some intentional work to keep myself from hardening. I had to declare, "I am not living in this swampland anymore. I choose to go through all my stuff, decide what's worth keeping, pack up my emotional wagon, and move out of here." It was a helluva lot of work, but the work got easier because I had become so clear about what mattered and who I was determined to become.

As I knew better, I could do better. I appreciated seeing my growth reflected back to me in positive relationships and experiences. People noticed the change in me and acknowledged it. My outcomes started changing—the work was working. I didn't focus on winning and losing anymore; I looked for win-wins. And people in relationships that mattered appreciated the difference.

When you take ownership and recognize your ability to change, it can feel like a challenge at first. But it can also bring about enormous self-trust and confidence. You make small promises to yourself to align with a new way of thinking. As you speak and act from that new place, you gain the confidence to do things you never thought possible. You access new parts of yourself that have the strength to do hard things.

Mindsets That Keep Us Stuck in Emotional Swampland

If you've ever felt trapped in the emotional muck of your past traumas, you can probably point the finger at several common negative mindsets. We all find ourselves subscribing to these narratives at some point, so let's examine them through the lens of agency to see what value we can extract.

"I'll never heal from this." Drew's loss was such a big, painful event in my life that I almost took on his death as my identity. I allowed his accident, and everything that came after, to become a statement of who I was: the mother who fell asleep, the mom everyone pitied at school. Especially when our pain feels undeserved, we can feel almost eager to put on the Cloak of Betrayal or the Cloak of Grief. I have seen bereaved parents lose themselves to gambling, substance abuse issues, and other addictions. I have seen them continue to punish themselves and never leave the cycle of suffering. Once we assume that cloak, it feels nearly impossible to take it off.

Part of owning our contribution to our pain is recognizing when we are holding onto it and when we need to let it go. However, letting go can feel threatening. Sometimes we resist letting go because we fear it means abandoning the memory of the person we lost. Other times, we hold on because the pain provides us with some small source of comfort or familiarity. Sometimes our pain becomes our justification for when things break down. But staying in the pain does not serve us. A pain-focused mind spirals us deeper into the coulda-shoulda-wouldas instead of reaching for the tools of transformation. By owning our pain, we also claim our ability to heal it.

You don't have to live in the pain. You can use the pain for something else. Or you can let it go. You get to choose.

"It's not my fault." It's easy to get stuck in blame mode—to see everyone else as the source of our continuing pain and struggle. *If they would be different, then I could be happy. If they would just stop, I wouldn't have to be this way.* I get it. I do. But no matter how long we fight it, healing is an inside-out job. Inner work changes our experiences in the outer world—not the other way around.

We lose time and agency getting hung up on what another person will or won't do for us in order for us to feel a certain way—happy, respected, loved. But to feel that way, we don't need other people to be different; we need to express and enforce our expectations and boundaries in a healthy, productive way. Then we can choose how to handle their response. If they respect our boundaries and expectations, great. And if not, we must find the willingness to say, "If this behavior doesn't change, I will take this specific action."

Admitting you're contributing to your own unhappiness takes courage. But the point isn't to beat yourself up—it's to bravely face the mirror, acknowledge the parts you would rather avoid, and let them be loved anyway. We cannot change or heal what we refuse to confront.

"I don't want to." Sometimes we allow ourselves to stay stuck in a negative situation because we're not ready to do the work required to change it. We can't pick every card handed to us, which can feel

CHAPTER 14: OWNERSHIP

downright cruel and unfair. *I didn't break it, so why should I have to be the one to pick up the shattered pieces?* We can be hurt so deeply that we come to believe our pain is the justification for the rest of our lives—how we think, act, and make choices moving forward. Our pain is very real. So for a while, we tend to pick what is easy instead of what is needed. The truths we avoid become the muck that pulls us deeper. At some point, the pain becomes insufferable, and our circumstances become intolerable. Fed up, we are finally ready for change.

You won't get there overnight, but you will get there.

• • •

Taking radical ownership of your life and choices can change everything. This kind of agency can open you up to emotional freedom, unshakable personal integrity, healthy boundaries, an empowered belief system, and a commitment to self-discovery that creates space for your authentic self. Fortunately, it also frees you from the stinky swampland of your most damaging narratives. That doesn't necessarily mean you'll never see swampland again. You'll almost certainly step in it a time or two and maybe pay it an extended visit. But eventually you'll ask, "What do I need in order to let this go?" Then you can listen, allow, and take the first step toward that beautiful horizon.

What Helped Me: Ownership Road Map

Once you find the awareness and courage to take ownership and challenge your negative patterns, the next question is: How? The tools in Part 2 of this book, along with others, may help as you upend old beliefs and embrace your autonomy to change them. Basic self-care will also help as you make yourself a priority. Most importantly, show yourself grace and compassion while avoiding judgment at all costs. Shame will only sink you further in the muck.

As with most of the healing journey, the exact path is for you to determine, but here I share the basic road map I used to take ownership and leave swampland in my rearview mirror. I included two examples for you: one that reflects my experience described in this chapter and another that addresses someone who feels stuck in a toxic friendship, something I see commonly with clients. As with much of this type of reflection, you may find your journal to be a safe place to capture your thoughts.

As I mentioned earlier, I don't often recommend *why* questions because they are focused on the past, but sometimes they are useful when we need to observe. So start with a *why*: Why is this painful? Why am I still attached to it? My example: "I realize that I am holding onto anger because it feels safer than vulnerability. The anger protects me from facing the sadness and fear of rejection underneath. Staying in my frustration allows me to avoid deeper insecurities about whether I am 'enough.'" Friendship example: "I constantly feel drained and unappreciated in this friendship."

Follow up each *why* question with a *how* or *what* question. What have I surrendered that I need to reclaim? How have I contributed

CHAPTER 14: OWNERSHIP

to the situation? My example: "For some reason, I have given up trusting my instincts. I have not set boundaries with people who disrespect me or leave me feeling overwhelmed." Friendship example: "I realize I let my friend talk about their problems all the time, and they rarely ask about mine. We feel out of balance in terms of our mutual support, our give and take."

Once you understand the negative pattern, cycle, or reaction you want to change, try to find a positive takeaway—even if it is merely gratitude for the new awareness. Flip your mindset from powerlessness to empowerment by taking ownership of what you can do to change this pattern. My example: "My outbursts are pushing people away. I can change that by remembering that my emotions are signals, not weapons. If I listen to them instead of unleashing them, I can strengthen my relationships." Friendship example: "I haven't set clear boundaries, and as a result, I often ignore the red flags I see because I don't want to cause conflict."

Finally, decide how you will respond next time you face this dynamic or cycle. Remember, you might not get it right the first time—or the twelfth time. You are not starting over each time though; you are simply starting better. My example: "Instead of snapping at someone who upsets me, I will pause and say, 'I need a moment to think about this.' I think this will help me feel more in control of my reactions." Friendship example: "I will have an honest conversation with my friend about my need for balance, and I will limit how much time I spend on their problems."

Approach these questions with radical honesty. This is the time to be raw and dig to get to the root of the issue and find some answers.

• •

CHAPTER FIFTEEN
NARRATIVES

Dear Drew,
Your spirit inspires me to be brave
as I navigate this journey.
Love, Mom

AFTER DREW'S ACCIDENT, Joey and I separated, but we found our way back to each other about a year later. It took a lot of forgiveness, but we both wanted to heal our family. Eventually, we also decided we wanted to try for another baby.

With my boys, I had no issues conceiving, but this time around, we had little luck. The doctors could not pinpoint a medical reason for my difficulty and suggested in vitro fertilization (IVF) as the next step. On paper, I was an excellent candidate; while the typical patient was in her forties, I was a healthy thirty-year-old with no underlying conditions or risk factors. The doctors expected an easy process, so when the first round of IVF came back with less-than-promising results, they called it a fluke. We adjusted the process and went for round two. But my body did not respond to the treatments—another failed attempt.

Over a period of four years, I did nine rounds of IVF. Each round required twice-daily injections of hormones, which I learned to administer myself. My body reacted to the medicine, developing large, painful red welts at the injection sites. Each time I went through egg-retrieval procedures and embryo transfers, we would get our hopes up, only to receive more bad news.

I got pregnant three times through IVF, and I lost each one. My third pregnancy made it to twenty-two weeks, when the rate of pregnancy loss drops to less than 1 percent, so I thought we had made it past the danger zone. We knew it was a boy and had started picking out names. We had also shared the happy news with family and friends. But my water spontaneously broke, and I went into labor. There was no saving the pregnancy.

As I sat in the hospital bed mourning yet another loss, I fell right back into the grief of losing Drew. *Why? What is it about me? Am I not meant to have children?* In that moment, I felt a little picked on by God. I started to reconsider the idea that maybe I was being punished for Drew's death. Maybe I really was a bad mom, and this was God's way of telling me to stop trying for another baby.

I knew I had to say no to that punishing narrative once and for all. I did not deserve a lifetime of pain and shame. God was not punishing me. I was a good mother. The truth is that accidents can happen to anyone. I could sit there begging God to tell me why he took my Drew, but some questions will never have satisfactory answers. So I chose my own answer: "No matter what anyone else thinks, I am allowed to say I am a good mother. I loved my son with all my heart. I would have done anything to keep him safe. I refuse to condemn myself to a lifetime of misery and shame based on an accident. That is not a sentence I am willing to serve."

It felt so good to know that my deepest pain did not have to be my truth.

My thoughts and fears did not instantly disappear after I decided to believe I was a good mother. I knew I had to consciously take charge of my inner narrative if I wanted to find the strength to keep trying for another baby. So I let my *no* get louder. Each time a punishing narrative entered my mind, I confronted it confidently—almost defiantly—and replaced it with an alternative belief. I repeated the truth I knew in my bones. I trusted my heart and let its warmth radiate through me. It took practice, but it worked.

After I left the hospital, I decided I was done with IVF. Within a few months, I got pregnant again, this time with no complications. With each of my IVF pregnancies, nothing had gone according to plan: I was bleeding, on bed rest, and perpetually anxious. But this pregnancy felt different, peaceful. I didn't even have morning sickness. I knew this baby would be born.

When we found out we were having a girl, all the suffering suddenly made sense to me: We were meant to have a daughter. Joey and Devin (now seven) were over the moon. A girl was a totally new adventure for our family, and even before her birth, she lifted our spirits and helped us turn the page together. My capacity for joy expanded again, big enough to make room for this beautiful little girl. After she was born, I remember whispering, "I understand now," as I rocked her in the nursery. For the first time in a long time, there was no bitterness, just sweetness.

We named her Hope.

When we choose the quality of our thoughts, beliefs, feelings, and stories, we claim the power to change them.

There is a moment in every trauma when we begin to tell ourselves a story. We don't receive the love and affection we desire from our parents, so the story becomes *You are unlovable*. We experience violence at the hands of those who are supposed to care for us, and our trauma says, *You deserve this*. We are touched too many times by loss and rejection, and each trauma chapter proves *Everybody leaves*.

If we are not present enough to notice the story that is being written, then it will eventually guide our lives like an invisible script—and we will call it fate. Triggers will continue to make old stories feel like present truths, and without an intentional choice to question them, they do become true for us, catching us in a cycle that feels inescapable.

We have the power to take back the pen and rewrite the story on our own terms, but first we must understand how our internal narratives are formed; only then can we uncover moments of agency for changing them.

The Formation of Narratives

Our thoughts, beliefs, and emotions build to form internal narratives—the stories we tell ourselves—that influence our choices and eventually shape the outcomes of our lives. For instance, we fail an exam and feel incompetent. We start thinking, *I'm so stupid*. Then our experiences after this thought appear as evidence: *Dad said that was a dumb question. My teacher doesn't think I can handle this class. I didn't get the job.* When one or more life experiences seem to reinforce negative thoughts, those thoughts become beliefs. My narrative, which stemmed from my childhood, was that I needed to be perfect or else I was a failure. Since I wasn't perfect in protecting Drew, I believed that I deserved the punishment I experienced with IVF.

When I use the term *narrative*, I mean both the stories we tell and the feelings, thoughts, and beliefs that contribute to those stories. Note that the formation of narratives is not necessarily a linear progression. Thoughts, beliefs, and feelings all influence one another. Feelings can cause thoughts; thoughts can reinforce feelings; deeply held beliefs can influence thoughts and feelings.

Our beliefs are at the core of everything we think, feel, and do. They shape the stories we tell ourselves; they influence our choices, behaviors, and patterns—often with a heavy hand—and form our core values and worldviews. Our beliefs often determine the trajectory of our lives because they make up the floor and ceiling of our perceived capabilities. They can be pernicious in what they compel us to do and what they keep us from trying. Sometimes our beliefs work in our favor, and sometimes they work against us. Throughout the healing process, it is our job to discern which belief does which.

But here's the problem: Our brains would rather be *right* about a *wrong* belief than be *wrong* and learn to accept a *right* belief. It is easier for our minds to accept the untrue belief *I am stupid* than it is to consider that we might actually be pretty smart. In fact, our brains have a natural tendency to seek out and interpret information that supports our current belief system; it has an inherent mechanism for confirmation bias. If I believe I am stupid, then I might not apply for a dream job, insisting that I am not qualified. For me, it would have been impossible for anyone to talk me out of IVF (and trust me, they tried), even after we'd reached the painful point when most people would have stopped. That's how deep my belief was that I had failed Drew—if I succeeded in having another baby, that would prove I was worthy of a second chance.

Regardless of how our beliefs serve us, they show up in the things we choose and the things we don't choose until they become a guiding theme we cannot seem to escape.

Our beliefs typically come from one of two places: the *cultural self*, the person our mind tells us we need to be to receive love and acceptance, or the *authentic self*, the person our heart tells us we are divinely created to become.

When we are asked what we believe, our mind typically answers first with beliefs we have been taught: beliefs that come from other people's opinions, our major life experiences, and difficult things that happen to us. These outside influences make up our cultural self, and they can include parental guidance, cultural upbringing, family traditions, socioeconomic conditions, geographical location, religious influences, education, and societal norms. Many of these learnings are good and legitimate, but when you take on what other people believe, those beliefs shape your opinion of yourself too. And sometimes the things you have been taught to believe about yourself are not actually true.

We can choose our beliefs with our minds, or we can dig deeper and ask: What does my *heart* tell me is true? By following our hearts, we can find our way back to the authentic self. The authentic self is what we might call our divine self. It is how God (the universe, the divine, the Love—choose your own language) would see us. It says things like *you are worthy, you are loved, you are whole*. Even if we were told terrible things—*you are unwanted, you are stupid, you are not enough*—the heart always knows the truth.

Testing Our Narratives

We must learn to test our narratives to discern where certain messages originate and whether they are true or false.

Imagine a teacher standing at the front of the classroom with a projector. The room's lights are dimmed, and the projector casts a beam of light onto a blank screen. The teacher holds up a small object in front of the projector. The students can't see the object, only its shadow on the screen. First, the teacher holds the object in one direction and asks, "What shape do you see?"

"Circle!" the students reply confidently.

Then, the teacher turns the object. "What shape do you see now?"

"Rectangle!"

Finally, the teacher turns on the lights to reveal the object. The students can now clearly see that the object is not a circle or a rectangle. It's a cylinder, a three-dimensional object that can cast either a circular or rectangular shadow depending on its orientation.

Sometimes what we see seems true, but until we have all the facts or a clearer perspective, we might see only one piece of the truth. Likewise, our narratives often appear to reveal "truths" that offer an incomplete picture.

Our thoughts, beliefs, feelings, and stories are not facts. Not every thought and feeling we have is true. Many of our emotions are triggered by negative thoughts and beliefs that are painfully *un*true. If someone thinks, *I am not good enough, I am not attractive enough, I am a failure*, those thoughts create an inaccurate picture of them, and yet they likely influence their beliefs, feelings, and choices. That is why it is so important to stop and ask: Is this thought or belief true for me, or is it something I was taught?

Since we cannot always determine the absolute "truth" of a situation, I like to define my thoughts and beliefs by the effect they have on me: empowering, disempowering, or neutral. A neutral thought or belief is typically something we cannot change, such as *It's raining outside,* or something that doesn't necessarily impact us emotionally, such as *We're having chicken for dinner.*

When distinguishing the difference between empowering and disempowering thoughts and beliefs, I focus on the feeling.

Disempowering thoughts and beliefs feel depleting, constricting, threatening, and destabilizing. They tend to cause emotional shutdown, crippling fear, self-doubt, and a defeatist attitude. Unfortunately, disempowering thoughts and beliefs often lead to self-sabotage and opportunities for further victimization because we are more likely to accept harmful behavior from others when we don't value ourselves. Disempowering beliefs typically come from our most traumatic life events and the hurtful words of others, and then they are stored as truth by our mind and the cultural self.

Conversely, empowering thoughts and beliefs feel renewing, expansive, uplifting, and supportive. They open our eyes to positive meaning, deep gratitude, and new perspectives. Stemming from the authentic self, empowering beliefs speak with the voice of the heart. Most importantly, they lead to outcomes that align with our ideal vision of the future.

Thoughts and beliefs themselves are not inherently good or bad, but they do influence our emotions, behavior, and well-being. For example, a belief like *I'm independent* might feel empowering for someone who values self-reliance, but it could be disempowering if it leads to difficulty asking for help. The belief *I need structure to succeed* might feel supportive to someone who thrives on routine but could feel stifling if it creates rigidity or resistance to change.

Understanding the difference between empowering and disempowering thoughts and beliefs can seem arduous. Especially after a lifetime of living according to a particular set of core beliefs, seeing them for what they are can be formidable, confusing, and maybe alarming. Here's the key: Beliefs either expand us or block us. They either keep us in alignment with our higher authentic self, or they knock us out of alignment and into our conditioned cultural self. They are either false opinions from outside us or the voice of wisdom within us. And you can feel the difference.

However, one of the biggest lessons I have learned on my healing journey is that feelings are not facts. They are *real*, yes. You do feel them, and they deserve to be acknowledged. But they are not necessarily absolute truth. In fact, many of our emotions stem from thoughts and beliefs that are *un*true.

Let's take a brief example: Your spouse comes home late without letting you know. You feel rejected and think, *They don't care about our family.* You can test that feeling with a simple analysis:

- **Fact:** What is the objective event? "My spouse came home late without calling or texting."
- **Fiction:** What story are you creating about that event? "They don't care about me or the family."
- **Feeling:** Note your feelings that stem from that fiction: "I feel rejected, hurt, and unimportant."
- **Truth:** Challenge that story by asking for other potential truths: "My spouse had a busy day and lost track of time; a colleague had an emergency; my spouse's phone died."

Instead of focusing on feelings of rejection, you can acknowledge the fact of the lateness and follow up with curiosity or compassion rather than anger. This process can help in distinguishing between what's real and what's an interpretation, guiding us toward a more balanced perspective. This is a simple example, but the same process works in more complex or painful situations.

I reiterate: Facts are not feelings. For the longest time, this tripped me up in my healing process. I believed that something could not be true if I didn't *feel* it—and if I felt it, it *must* be true. I had to learn to change my thoughts in order to change my feelings. Again, all the narrative elements influence one another.

CHOOSING OUR NARRATIVES

If our thoughts, beliefs, feelings, and stories are not facts, then they are choices. We can decide what types of feelings and emotions we want to pursue; we can choose to practice thinking differently; we can determine what we believe about ourselves, others, and the world.

Choosing to take on the belief *I'm a bad mother* would have closed me off to having more children—and it wasn't true. Choosing to do the work to change my belief system and its associated narratives was uncomfortable, but believing that I was an unworthy mother was worse. When I made the intentional choice to start believing something that felt good—even if I did not yet know it was true—I was accepting that my belief was, in fact, a choice.

When we accept our thoughts, beliefs, emotions, and stories as choices, we claim the power to change them. We discover a new source of agency in the healing process. Each time one of those disempowering narratives creeps in, we can recognize the moment of agency and say, "No, I believe something else."

Once we have done that, we have tapped into another incredible truth: Our thoughts, beliefs, feelings, and stories aren't fixed; we can redesign them at any time. Our inner narratives are not carved in stone. They are written and rewritten as we evolve as human beings. Once we see that the pen has been in our hands the whole time, we can start writing something worth reading.

Interrupting Our Narrative Patterns

We can redesign our thought patterns and belief systems by interrupting our inner narratives with intentional action. There are plenty of ways to do this. Affirmations can disrupt a thought and cut off a negative narrative at the root. When we expose ourselves to new perspectives—varying our social circles, taking a class, traveling someplace new—we are more likely to open ourselves up to change. Sometimes changing our environment can cause a big adjustment in our emotions: taking a walk, revisiting an old haunt, or sitting in a cafe. Simple routine shifts also help—like taking a break from friends that activate our *I'm not good enough* wound, unfollowing social media accounts that trigger our *My life is not fancy enough* belief, and getting up every morning and high-fiving ourselves in the mirror.

Pattern interruption takes practice, and changing decades of deep-rooted narratives requires consistent action. You cannot think your way through this one, or you will get stuck somewhere between a negative thought and the disempowering choice that follows. Learning to interrupt narrative patterns and redesign belief systems can be—I hate to say it—tedious. It is a slow and methodical practice more often than it is a rapid breakthrough. So practice noticing your thoughts. Ask yourself if they feel empowering, disempowering, or neutral. Take a moment to understand where your beliefs come from, and then, if needed, choose more empowered beliefs. The reshaping process requires a clear choice—over and over. So stay the course and focus on consistency. The narrative will begin to change. And the best part is *you* get to change with it.

What Helped Me: Belief Alignment Reflection

Do you know that feeling when your gut tells you to do one thing but you go against it and do something else? There is a disconnect, a misalignment, discord between intuition and action. When I get that sort of gut feeling, I have learned that it is often an indicator that I have some belief that is not aligned with my authentic self. Reflective journaling helps me identify that belief so I can test it and decide what to do with it. This practice allows me to bring my beliefs into alignment with my authentic self, and my subsequent decisions reflect that harmony.

If you are ready to start exploring your beliefs, grab a notebook and pen, and carve out some time to reflect. This practice can take a very short amount of time for a specific situation, but it may take hours or days or even years for deeply embedded beliefs and complex issues. So if you don't get to an answer in one sitting, don't worry—you can come back to this practice regularly. I find it is key to have uninterrupted time and a quiet mind, so you might try a meditation or grounding practice first.

First, identify whether there is a specific situation or gut feeling you are considering. List the beliefs you hold about yourself and the situation. If you don't have something specific on your mind, you can also reflect more generally about your beliefs. Who do you believe you are? Example: "I am resilient," "I am a failure," or "I am unworthy." Write down what comes to mind, positive or negative.

Look at each belief and decide whether it is empowering or disempowering. If you find this difficult to determine, reposition your awareness to the underlying emotion. What emotion is driving this belief? Does it trigger you or expand you? If it feels good, then let that be enough. If it feels bad, then let it go.

When you identify a disempowering belief, consider whether you have evidence it might not be true and what alternative beliefs would feel empowering and true.

Finally, consider: If you were living fully from your authentic self, what would your beliefs about yourself and this situation look like? How would your life change?

Your gut feelings indicate some part of you is trying to be heard. Give yourself a pause to listen.

CHAPTER SIXTEEN

MEANING

Dear Drew,
You have taught me so much about resilience
that I will carry forever.
Love, Mom

YEARS AFTER learning about Joey's affair, I found out it wasn't a one-time thing. His infidelity had continued throughout the decade and a half we had been married. I felt like I'd been hit by an earthquake, and I spent months sitting in the aftermath, sifting through the wreckage. It took me a long time to process the betrayal. As I grappled with the raw emotion, toxic internal narratives quietly took root before I even realized they were there.

At first, it was incredibly tempting to blame myself. The familiar critical thoughts crept in almost immediately: *Is it my appearance? Am I not thin enough? Not young enough?* I started questioning everything about myself. *Why didn't he care about the harm his choices caused me?* I could hear the mutters, louder and louder: *No one will ever love you. You're not cherished. You're a fool.* Taking over, these internal narratives painted a picture of my worth that had nothing to do with reality but everything to do with how deeply the deceit cut.

Betrayal has a way of coaxing us into self-blame, convincing us we are somehow responsible for others' choices. The mind spins stories of shame and self-doubt, leaving us to feel small and unworthy. I certainly fell into this trap. The persuasive inner critic and incessant questioning sucked me in, and for a while it felt like I had wandered right back into the same emotional swamp I had mucked about in before.

But then I heard a faint whisper inside me: *It's not about you.* Slowly, the voice of my heart grew louder. *It's not about you.* I took a moment to consider whether Joey's choices really did reflect on my value or my worth. *His decisions are his own.* And just like that, the weight of those painful thoughts started to lift. Joey's cheating was about him—not me. He chose unfaithfulness, and I no longer needed to internalize his actions as a reflection of my shortcomings. Suddenly I felt the power and wisdom of my healing work returning. I refused to wear the cloak of his infidelity like an identity. It would not define me.

Of course I contributed to the struggles in our marriage. I wish I had done many things differently. Looking back, I can see where my willingness to strengthen the marriage fell short. But my contributions could go only so far if my partner stepped outside the marriage's core agreements. If he wanted something different from me, he could have brought that to my attention, to work on changing our dynamic. He could have taken ownership of his contribution and asked me to take ownership of mine. We could have rebuilt the marriage together before he decided to engage in affairs.

I had spent most of my life thinking that if someone didn't love me, then the fault lay with me. But by this point in my healing journey,

I had learned that feelings weren't facts, and I wasn't going down that road again. I would no longer allow others' opinions and actions to mean something about me. Of course other people's choices would still affect me, but they did not have to change how I valued myself. My husband's repeated infidelity did not mean that I didn't deserve faithful love; it meant I probably should have reevaluated the marriage sooner.

I learned from the experience. He chose his action, but I could choose my result. While we stayed together several more years for financial and child-related reasons, we did ultimately divorce. And I decided that no matter what happened to me, from there on out, I would determine what my life looked like.

WE CAN'T CHOOSE ALL OUR EXPERIENCES, BUT WE CAN CHOOSE WHAT THEY MEAN TO US.

Life is a story in which we don't always get to choose the plot points. Sometimes life throws us situations we never anticipated—betrayal, loss, heartbreak, and trauma. We feel a complete lack of control, like outside forces dictate our narrative. To complicate matters, sometimes we don't know the other characters as well as we thought.

But I've said it before, and I'll say it again: You are the author of your own story. You may not control how other people act or the events that happen to you, but you have the power to decide what those events mean to you and how they shape your life moving forward. You get to decide how your story develops. You get to turn the page. You can even close the book and start a new one.

We opened the discussion of narratives in the last chapter, and in this one, I want to deepen that discussion. Recall that while feelings, thoughts, and beliefs are *real*, they are not necessarily *facts*. We can test them and, if needed, change them; we can choose thoughts and beliefs that are empowering or disempowering. Once you realize this, you gain the ability to determine what is true—good, bad, or otherwise—and extract meaning from it in a way that empowers you.

The moment of agency is critical. If we don't recognize that moment, our subconscious chooses our narratives for us, and for various reasons—often to maintain the status quo—it likes to interpret things through a disempowering lens. Our significant other breaks up with us, and we think, *I'm so stupid. Other people aren't safe. No one will ever love me.* Then we allow that interpretation to affect our behavior moving forward: *I'm so stupid—but I won't ever be fooled again. Other people aren't safe—so I can never fully relax in a romantic relationship. No one will ever love me—so I give up on love.* One negative experience can snowball into a lifetime of disempowering and potentially misguided choices because we missed the moment to choose a different story.

By contrast, when we intentionally choose an empowering interpretation to use as we move forward, we almost immediately broaden our capability and options: *We weren't the right fit—I will keep looking for someone who shares my values and interests. I was never quite comfortable with that person—so now I know that my feelings of safety are a good indicator of suitability. The right person will show up at the right time—and in the meantime I will enjoy life and continue developing myself.*

Two powerful complementary tools have helped me rewrite my most painful narratives: intentional interpretation and applied meaning.

Intentional Interpretation and Applied Meaning

Intentional interpretation is a framework for understanding the original intent behind beliefs, actions, or events in order to gain clarity and reframe our perspective. Rather than passively accepting the default interpretation that our subconscious supplies, this approach empowers us to actively choose our interpretation of a particular experience.

We begin by reflecting on the origin of the beliefs or feelings associated with a particular experience. If the experience involves someone else's actions, we consider their possible intentions and how that aligns with our own interpretation. Given that context, we can then reframe our understanding into a more empowering interpretation.

For my situation with Joey, I felt unworthy because he cheated on me. That feeling stemmed from a belief that I could make my marriage work by being a good partner. But if I looked at Joey's intention, I could see the truth: His infidelity reflected his struggles with commitment and his love of "the chase." That allowed me to reframe my interpretation: Joey's infidelity was about his choice, not about my value or worth. My worth is unrelated to anyone else's actions. This intentional shift in perspective became key to accessing my agency and moving forward with clarity.

Applied meaning is how we use whatever interpretation we adopt. It is how our interpretation shows up in our feelings or behavior. It is both an action and a way of being, and by assigning new, empowering meaning to past experiences, we can foster growth and healing. In this process, we reflect on a painful situation to assess what it means to us currently; then we brainstorm to find a new, empowering meaning and decide how we can apply it to our actions going forward.

For my situation with Joey, I felt like I wasn't good enough; I allowed his betrayal to mean that I was unlovable and undeserving of loyalty. In looking for new meaning, I realized I could take a valuable lesson from the experience: It is important to set boundaries and value myself. From there, I could decide to prioritize relationships that entailed mutual respect and aligned with my self-worth.

When we see our agency, we can interpret even our toughest experiences through an empowering lens. We can methodically process trauma in a way that heals instead of hardens, learning more about ourselves and how we want to move through grief. Agency gives us a sense of control and stability even when we can't entirely choose what happens to us. Unanswered questions feel less threatening as we begin deciding which answers serve us.

Drew's passing was probably the most extreme example of my choice to find meaning in an experience I never would have asked for. Once the accident happened, I could either look at it as the day that destroyed my life, or I could choose to see it as a touchpoint of revelation—revealing to me the fragility of his life, the finality of his death, and the gratitude I felt to have had the chance to love Drew at all.

Today, I continue to use intentional interpretation to get through a crisis or past trauma because it creates the opportunity to expand my perspective and choose my next step with meaning—and it feels so much better than the alternative.

Potential Lessons to Watch For

Of course, learning to find empowering interpretations in deeply painful experiences takes time and effort—it is rarely obvious or easy.

CHAPTER 16: MEANING

Feeling stuck in the muck of grief or anger is natural, and you won't find all the answers right away. I reiterate: healing is not a straight line—it is the process of discovering how to give new meaning to the most difficult chapters of life.

But even when your pain feels futile and purposeless, you can find lessons buried there, lessons that can propel you toward a better future. You can:

Learn your boundaries. Trauma teaches us what we will and will not accept. After enduring painful situations, we become more attuned to our inner compass and develop a clearer sense of where our limits lie. We learn what is nonnegotiable. For instance, after a toxic relationship, you might learn to say, "I will never tolerate dishonesty again." Your boundaries become a powerful form of self-respect.

Learn who you don't want to become. Sometimes, the people who hurt us also model for us who we *don't* want to be. If you were treated unfairly at work, you can use that experience to delineate things you will or won't do. For example, you may decide that you don't want to be like your boss and that you will treat colleagues with respect. That lesson becomes a source of strength, not something that holds you in the past.

Learn the power of vulnerability. Most of us struggle with vulnerability, especially when we have been hurt. But through the pain, you may discover the beauty of letting your guard down again, this time with someone who will cherish your heart. Gratitude for vulnerability can be an empowering result of deep emotional wounds. If you open yourself to love, you show that you are stronger than the fear that once held you back.

Rebuild a sense of self-worth. Often after trauma, we feel small or undeserving of love and happiness. By rewriting your story and finding new interpretations of your experiences, you can affirm your inherent value. Instead of thinking, *I was unworthy of loyalty,* you might tell yourself, *I am worthy of respect, honesty, and love.* That simple adjustment can change everything.

Find resilience. Pain is a teacher. It reveals our strength. We discover that we can get through tough times even when we feel broken. Each time you pick yourself up, you deepen your understanding of your own strength.

Acknowledging Resistance and the Dangers of Toxic Positivity

Even when we see a new, empowering interpretation of our trauma, we often resist accepting it. Shifting our mindset and choosing an empowering interpretation can feel unnatural, like we're trying to minimize our pain. We might hear the voice of self-doubt: *Who do you think you are? You're being naive. You can't "choose" to feel better.* Your past wounds might flare up, demanding acknowledgment. Let them; old wounds naturally get louder when we try to change the narrative around them. Recognize that healing is not an instant fix—it is a practice that takes time.

However, it is also important to pay attention to your resistance and question whether you are facing "toxic positivity"—the pressure to always find a silver lining or push yourself to "move on." That mindset is not helpful, and it does not honor your pain. Feeling sad, angry, or confused after trauma or a painful experience is *normal.* Emotions like grief or fear are not problems that require fixing but rather signals that you are processing something deep and meaningful.

Remember, intentional interpretation does not mean you bypass your feelings; instead, it asks you to acknowledge the pain without letting it define you. *I see you, I feel you, and I choose to create positive meaning from you.*

• • •

You are a powerful creator, capable of taking the deepest pain and transforming it into something meaningful. Life will throw challenges your way, but you don't have to let those challenges define you. You don't have to surrender your story or your worth to anyone else's limitations. You get to choose the meaning.

So look for a positive interpretation. Look for the lesson, the strength, the opportunity for growth. When something bad happens, acknowledge it, accept it, and then decide what you want it to mean in your life. Don't let your deepest fears or traumas write the next chapter for you. You are the author. The pen is in your hands.

What Helped Me: Integrated Framework for Intentional Interpretation and Applied Meaning

Rewriting narratives takes practice, and intentional interpretation and applied meaning are two of the most powerful tools I have found for myself. I share them with people regularly. Here, I am offering an abbreviated, integrated framework that brings the two concepts together; on my website (melissahull.com), you can find expanded, step-by-step guides. Either approach can help you create a cohesive and empowering narrative for healing–choose the level of detail that works best for you.

Once you've identified a situation, event, or experience you wish to work on, go through the following steps:

1. **Reflect on the event's original context.** Ask yourself: What did I originally believe about this event? What might have been the other person's intention (if applicable)? Example: "I believed my worth depended on being loved by my husband."
2. **Acknowledge the impact.** Write down how this event has shaped your thoughts, feelings, or actions. Example: "It made me question my value and avoid vulnerability."
3. **Choose a new interpretation.** Use intentional interpretation to clarify the event's origins, and apply meaning to reshape its influence on your life. Ask yourself: What truth can I uncover about this experience, and how can I use it to empower myself? Example: "This event taught me that my worth is inherent, not dependent on others' actions."
4. **Integrate the new narrative.** Create a statement or affirmation that reflects the empowering meaning. Example: "I am worthy of love and respect, and I will honor that truth in all my relationships."
5. **Take action aligned with the new meaning.** Identify one tangible action you can take to live out this new interpretation. Example: "I will seek out healthy, supportive relationships or practice self-care that affirms my value."

Practice, practice, practice this framework, and as you rewrite the narrative of your life, you will see your story unfold in beautiful ways.

CHAPTER SEVENTEEN
EMPATHY

Dear Drew,
I still see the way you'd run to me
with arms outstretched after every scraped knee,
trusting I could make it better.
Love, Mom

MY FATHER WORKED HARD to support us. He provided for us single-handedly despite incredible pressure and adversity. I'll always be grateful for his diligence and sacrifice, but not all the lessons he taught were worthy of carrying forward. I remember as a kid thinking of my father as an empty well. If I needed emotional support, I could never throw my bucket down and have any hope of it coming up full.

My dad was a man of few words, and he kept his emotions under tight wrap. He didn't know how to give me what I needed emotionally, and the distance between us grew palpable. I took on the pain of that distance as part of my self-image, my behavior, and my parenting. For the longest time I couldn't even entertain the idea that I might be mirroring my father's harmful behaviors, but when I could hide from myself no longer, I chose differently. As I shared earlier, I started working with a parenting coach, and I didn't hold back in describing my history, my own unwanted behaviors, and my fears about where they might lead.

In reprocessing my childhood with professional guidance, I finally saw clearly that I did not do anything wrong as a child; I did not carry the responsibility of resolving my parents' adult problems. The treatment I received wasn't right, and it wasn't my fault. As I mourned for the little girl I once was, I could feel my empathy grow for both her and my adult self. After decades of feeling inherently defective or unlovable, I learned to care for my inner child the way I wanted to care for my own children. Once I understood my painful childhood experiences in a new context, they no longer triggered me and instead became a source of strength, a wellspring of resilience I could draw on.

As I viewed my childhood through a lens of compassion, I began to see my dad differently too. His own childhood had been vastly more difficult than mine, and as I worked through my anger, I came to understand how he could have struggled too. Overwhelmed, exhausted, and dealing with my mother's illness, he lacked the support and resources needed to handle the demands of fatherhood. He did the best he could with the tools he had, but he had no access to the emotional parts of himself.

How could I expect to get something from him that he couldn't get from himself?

CHAPTER 17: EMPATHY

Nothing justified his harmful behavior, but because I had learned to recognize my own humanness, I caught a glimpse of his as well. If I could allow myself to grow and evolve, then I should be able to do the same for him.

I knew I needed to forgive my dad for the past, but I also knew he wasn't open to hearing me out and probably never would be. I would have loved for us to have an honest, healing conversation, but talking to him would not result in the kind of resolution I wanted for us both. Instead, I decided to approach my childhood pain as something I could release on my own. I wrote him a letter, pouring everything I ever wanted or needed to say onto paper so that I could stop reliving it. Then I burned the letter. As I watched the words go up in flames, I let them carry the pain away along with the smoke. I did it again and again as emotions continued to come up for me. Eventually, I forgave him. I let the past go. I chose to love us both the way he never could.

My ability to move beyond the pain of my childhood changed radically the minute I stopped needing that conversation with my dad. I brought myself closure without requiring his participation or approval—a new experience for me. Over time, as I continued my commitment to difficult emotional work, the past no longer held me hostage. I could no longer be injured by what my father wouldn't or couldn't give me. I learned to love him where he was, and I recognized that I had the capacity to love in ways I had never received.

Today I see my father with more tenderness and empathy than I ever thought possible. And by letting the past go, I made room for what I truly wanted: love, peace, and compassion.

BY ACCEPTING OUR OWN HUMANNESS, WE OPEN THE DOOR TO EMPATHY, ALLOWING US TO SEE AND ACCEPT THE HUMANNESS IN OTHERS.

Empathy is the ability to understand and share another's feelings. It is both a skill and an art, rooted in awareness and fueled by a sense of connection. Empathy goes beyond imagining what another person might feel; it requires us to hold space for their experience without judgment or the need to "fix" them. In the context of healing, empathy acts as a bridge—connecting us to ourselves, others, and the broader human experience. By practicing empathy, we begin to soften the emotional walls built by pain, allowing healing to unfold in a way that fosters deeper self-awareness and connection.

Empathy begins within. By extending kindness and understanding to ourselves, we create a foundation for extending the same compassion to others. As we discussed in Chapter 13, grace—self-empathy—invites us to view our experiences with curiosity rather than judgment, embracing our flaws and struggles not as failures but as essential parts of being human. Rather than think, *I always mess things up; I'm not good enough*, we can think, *This moment doesn't define my worth; it's an opportunity to grow*. This act of self-compassion not only eases our immediate pain but also nurtures resilience.

Once we extend grace to ourselves, we can practice extending empathy outwardly, starting with those closest to us. We've all been frustrated with someone, maybe a spouse, friend, or coworker. Perhaps they made a mistake or hurt us, and our immediate reaction was anger or resentment. What if instead of blaming them, we could pause and consider that they too are human? They might be wrestling with their own pain, fears, or insecurities. Imagine if in those moments we chose to meet others with empathy instead of judgment, repositioning from thinking *They shouldn't talk to me like that! They were the one who screwed up!* to *That was an unusual mistake; I wonder if something is going on with them.* This mindset does not mean excusing harmful behavior but rather recognizing that, like us, others are both flawed and capable of growth. By shifting our reactions toward empathy, we break the cycle of reactive pain and move toward intentional healing, not just for ourselves but for our relationships as well.

Learning to extend grace to others creates more peaceful relationships, less conflict, and a deeper connection with the people around us. Hard as it was, I learned to see even Joey with empathy and his choices for what they were: acts rooted in fear. He struggled to handle the aftermath of Drew's death and the dysfunction in our marriage, so instead, he pursued distractions—work, hobbies, affairs—to avoid looking at himself and his responsibility. Recognizing his fear, I could only empathize. This shift didn't excuse his behavior, but it did allow me to release the burden of resentment, freeing up emotional space for my own healing.

Who in your life might warrant some empathy? Take a moment to reflect on a recent interaction where you reacted with frustration or anger. Can you reframe that moment with empathy? What might have been going on beneath the surface? As you consider this, notice whether offering empathy also lightens your emotional burden.

Cultivating Empathy

As with most of the skills used in healing, empathy is not a one-time act but a daily practice that deepens with intention. To cultivate empathy, start with these three approaches.

Notice reactivity. We often react to others automatically—that is, without thinking—and as a result, unintentionally overlook the other person's humanity. By noticing our reactivity, we can see where we may be caught in old patterns of fear or anger. For instance, maybe you snap at someone close to you, or withdraw in silence instead of addressing an issue. When this happens, you can ask yourself: How could I have responded more empathetically? Perhaps you could have taken a deep breath, acknowledged your feelings without letting them control you, and responded more calmly. Observation and intention can help create new patterns that are rooted in compassion, understanding, and love. Each time we choose empathy over reactivity, we reinforce our own healing by proving to ourselves that we are no longer controlled by old wounds.

Listen empathetically. Empathetic listening involves being fully present with another person and their story without interrupting, judging, or offering solutions. It requires us not only to hear their words but also to attend to the emotions behind the words, and to reflect back our understanding. For example, if a friend shares that they feel overwhelmed at work, instead of saying, "You just need to set better boundaries," you might say, "That sounds really stressful. I can see why you're feeling this way." By validating the other person's feelings, we foster trust and reinforce their sense of being seen and heard, which is deeply healing. As we practice this, we help others feel understood and also deepen our own ability to receive empathy, creating a positive cycle of mutual support.

Practice perspective taking. Perspective taking is essentially putting yourself in another person's shoes to understand them. I have found two tactics especially useful for shifting my perspective.

First, before responding to someone, I like to pause to consider their emotions and experiences and ask: What might they be feeling right now? Second, I imagine myself in other people's situations, focusing on how I would feel if it were me—not on how I think they should feel. Both approaches can shift my perspective in a flash.

Healthy Empathy Versus Toxic Empathy

To maintain its transformative power, empathy requires balance. Healthy empathy allows us to understand the emotions of others while maintaining clear emotional boundaries. It encourages genuine connection by creating space for someone else's feelings without absorbing them as our own. For example, if a grieving friend expresses sadness, healthy empathy means listening with compassion and acknowledging their pain without trying to fix it. This type of empathy fosters mutual respect, understanding, and personal growth for both parties. When we set healthy emotional boundaries, we ensure that empathy enhances our healing rather than depletes us.

By contrast, toxic empathy occurs when the ability to share in someone's emotions becomes overbearing or unhealthy. It often manifests as becoming enmeshed in someone else's struggles or as taking on their pain so fully that it feels like our own. Toxic empathy, instead of providing support, often results in codependency, emotional burnout, and resentment. Constantly prioritizing another's needs at the expense of our own emotional health can create a cycle where neither person feels truly supported or healed. We deplete ourselves while unintentionally disempowering the person we're trying to help.

The distinction between healthy and toxic empathy lies in the presence—or absence—of emotional boundaries. Healthy empathy respects the individuality of both parties, fostering compassion while allowing each person to remain emotionally intact. With it, you support the other person's healing without diminishing your own emotional resources. Toxic empathy lacks these boundaries, resulting in enmeshment, emotional exhaustion, and an unhealthy dynamic.

Recognizing this difference is crucial but not always easy. A sibling loses a job and asks for some money to tide them over. Certainly, some emergency assistance might be warranted, but what happens when the sibling comes back repeatedly? Or an adult child drinks too much and makes a scene at a family holiday event. How many times do you forgive this type of behavior without establishing consequences? In the workplace, managers often get caught in a cycle of providing answers for employees rather than letting them seek solutions themselves; providing answers might be expedient initially, but it ultimately stunts the employees' professional growth. In all these examples, what starts as an act of kindness slides into coddling or enabling and potentially codependency.

Unfortunately, the relationships in which an unhealthy dynamic is most likely to emerge are our nearest relationships—family, friends, close colleagues—making the dynamic even trickier to unwind. By cultivating emotional awareness and boundaries, we can ensure that our empathy remains a source of strength and healing rather than harm.

If you have concerns about whether you are taking empathy too far, here are some tips:

Notice any signs of overidentification. If you walk away from a conversation feeling emotionally exhausted, anxious, or guilty for not "fixing" things, you have probably stepped into toxic empathy. The moment you feel responsible for someone else's healing, you have crossed the line.

Pause before absorbing. When someone shares their pain, take a breath. Instead of instinctively *feeling* their emotions as your own, ask yourself whether you are trying to support them, or trying to save them. Healthy empathy means witnessing, not carrying.

Check in with yourself. After an emotional conversation, ask yourself whether you are still carrying its weight. If the answer is yes, remind yourself it is not yours to hold. A simple moment of awareness can help release what doesn't belong to you.

We cannot do the healing work for someone else; we can only walk beside them as they do it, with love and boundaries in equal measure. Sometimes we must have tough conversations. Sometimes we must let people feel the consequences of their actions. Sometimes people will not be happy with us when we say no. We have to get used to not pleasing everyone in every situation. The real power of empathy is in witnessing. When we learn to hold space without losing ourselves, we create deeper, more honest connections both with others and with ourselves.

In a world often marked by disconnection and misunderstanding, empathy is a radical act of love and connection. It challenges us to move beyond our own perspective and embrace the humanity of others. In cultivating empathy, we foster healing in ourselves, we deepen our relationships, and we help create a more compassionate, connected world.

What Helped Me: Using Language to Empower Others

For years, I blurred the line between support and self-sacrifice, carrying emotions that weren't mine and mistaking enmeshment for care. To detangle myself from that dynamic, one of the most valuable tools I learned was shifting my language.

Instead of saying, "Let me help you figure this out," I now say something like "I trust you to handle this, and I'm here if you need support." Other examples you might try:
- "I believe in your ability to work through this."
- "That sounds really difficult. What do you think would help?"
- "I'm here to listen and support you."

Similarly, if someone comes up with an idea and asks for my opinion or advice, I am cautious in my language: "Here is what has worked for me in my situation. . . . I don't know if it will work for you in yours." While I might give examples or possibilities, I try to avoid telling someone what to do and instead reassure them they have the strength and capability to find their own answers.

These subtle changes in language can allow you to hold space without overstepping and to empathize while also encouraging the other person in their own personal growth. By using language that empowers others, we reinforce our own healing by setting boundaries and practicing emotional balance.

PART FOUR

Create a Life Bigger Than Grief

GRIEF FRACTURES YOUR WORLD into shards of memory, pain, and longing. At first, these fragments seem only to cut and wound, their edges too sharp to handle. But in time, you realize they are more than broken remnants of what was—they are the raw material for something new. You gather the heartaches, lessons, and moments of clarity that emerge from your loss, each fragment carrying its own truth. Slowly, you arrange the pieces, letting them settle into place like colorful bits in a kaleidoscope, trusting that they belong. This deliberate act demands the courage to let light illuminate what lies within. Turn the lens slightly, and the pattern shifts, interweaving beauty and chaos. Some days, the pattern appears blurred; others, it takes your breath away.

Eventually, you learn how to fuse the shards—not to erase their edges, but to transform them. What was once a shifting pattern of light and color solidifies into something both fluid and strong. You are no longer just observing the pieces—you are living them. They become part of you, deepening your capacity for joy, resilience, and purpose. One piece teaches you strength, another compassion; together, they reveal how love and loss can coexist. Like a piece of handblown glass, your life becomes an artful expression of your experience. It is beautiful, unique, and entirely yours.

This is how you create a life bigger than grief: picking up the pieces, placing them in your heart, and melding past and future into something new.

CHAPTER EIGHTEEN
SERVICE

Dear Drew,
I promise to keep your spirit alive
through acts of kindness and
sharing your story.
Love, Mom

ABOUT SIX MONTHS after Drew died, I was dropping off Devin at school, and a woman I had never met approached me with an audacious idea. She taught water safety to parents and children throughout the region, and she asked if I would join her. When it comes to water safety, she explained, most parents think about pools, lakes, and other large bodies of water. But in rural Arizona, additional dangers lurked: irrigation canals, water tanks, water troughs, and more. These were the quiet, hidden hazards that too often claimed lives without warning. In fact, according to the National Children's Center for Rural and Agricultural Health and Safety, drowning rates for all age groups are three times higher in rural areas than urban areas. Drew, for example, fell into an open irrigation canal that ran behind many of our neighbors' properties. As this woman reminded me of truths I knew too well, she said she thought I had a unique opportunity to make a difference.

At the time, I was still navigating the rawest waves of grief, but something about her proposal ignited a small spark within me. Asking a bereaved mother to talk about her most profound loss was a bold move, but I am so glad she did—because this single act of service helped save my life. It is also why, to this day, I believe wholeheartedly that serving others plays a crucial and powerful role in the healing process. In service, we find the threads of connection that grief so often severs. Though the idea of talking about my most painful experience terrified me, almost immediately I knew in my bones I had to do it. A typical water safety instructor could hold an audience for only so long, but Drew's story added credibility and intensity that truly captured people's attention. Stories connect us in ways statistics never can. By sharing, I could help spare other families from the pain I battled every day.

I felt a rush of uncertainty. What if it went wrong? Could I endure another setback? For a while, the answer was definitely no, I could not. However, after considering the meaning of this choice, I decided I could do it. With the right tools and mindset, this challenge could yield positive outcomes for me and the families in Yuma.

I spoke to schools, parent groups, and organizations throughout our entire county. Each time I shared Drew's story, I was not just recounting a tragedy—I was reclaiming my voice. Each time I talked about his accident, I became a little less scared of what my grief could do to me, and my resilience grew. I couldn't predict or prepare for every question, but with enough practice, I built trust in myself and confidence in my ability to show vulnerability again. Grief had

CHAPTER 18: SERVICE

taken much from me, but it didn't have to take my ability to create meaning.

The hardest classroom to visit was Drew's. Naturally, his preschool classmates had been asking where he had gone, and none of the adults knew how to answer. Everyone needed space to talk about it, and the kids had some tough questions. With innocent curiosity, one boy raised his hand and softly asked, "Do you think Drew knew he was dying?"

I had not prepared for that one.

To do this work, I had to become very comfortable with being uncomfortable. Instead of following my triggers down the rabbit hole, I focused on the grit I could feel building inside me each time I didn't crumble, each time I decided to keep going despite the pain. Every tough question, every devastating statistic, became proof that I could find strength in the greater good. I could feel it every time I stepped in front of an audience.

Over time, I saw the full impact of sharing Drew's story. Today, more than twenty years later, I still run into families I spoke to about water safety. They remember my story and advice as if I had shared it yesterday: "I never forgot what you told me." "I always remembered to wait for an adult before going near water." "I still think about Drew." "I have my own kids now, and I know how to protect them." One child from Drew's class reached out years later to say she had saved a younger family member because she knew to pay attention.

Everything came full circle for me. Service didn't erase my pain, but it gave it a purpose. It changed Drew's accident and the devastating fact that his life had been cut short into a legacy that needed sharing. Each testimony served as external evidence of the partnership I chose to create with Drew's life, to carry his story forward so it could mean more than just his death. Drew's story inspired a ripple effect that lives on, and it reaches so far, I don't know where it will end. That knowledge lit up my darkest days—and it still fuels me from one service project to the next. Grief doesn't have to be the end of the story; it can be the beginning of something profound.

Pain creates powerful opportunities to serve others—and ourselves.

In the midst of grief, it seems impossible that anything meaningful can come from our loss. Yet service work has a way of moving us away from devastation and toward healing. It doesn't erase the pain, but it does help channel it and transmute it. When I first took on speaking about water safety, I wanted to honor Drew's life, but I quickly realized that service work made my heart lift. It was an exchange: I was receiving as well as giving. While everyone's experience is different, some key aspects of service work help propel grievers out of pain and onto a more positive emotional trajectory.

Service inspires hope. Serving others can literally give you a reason to live. When you turn your focus on others, you begin to see what you can do instead of seeing only what happened to you. Whether your service is one of your regular volunteer activities or stems from the pain or trauma you have experienced, giving to others can lift you from hopelessness. Due to the nature of Drew's accident, I was called to service in a particularly visible way, but when I wasn't speaking regularly, I sought out small opportunities to create good in the world—buying someone's coffee, taking flowers to the nursing home, offering a few kind words to an overwhelmed mom at the grocery store—because they made me feel better. As much as they benefited others, they kept me going.

Service provides a sense of agency. One of the hardest things about grief is the sense of helplessness, the loss of control. Disempowerment can settle in because we simply don't know how to move forward with so much pain. What we eventually choose, however, can be either destructive or productive for us and others. Choosing service is choosing empowerment over despair. Participating in work that helps other people declares to yourself and the world that you choose a productive path for your pain. It repositions your focus from passive feelings of despair to active engagement in positive solutions.

Service offers stability. Taking part in service projects also helps create a sense of structure and routine, offering stability during a disorienting time. It anchors us when we feel lost. By making decisions, organizing tasks, and seeing tangible outcomes, we experience personal growth and rediscover our strengths, which boosts our confidence and self-worth. Service allows us to connect with others, build a support network, and avoid the isolation that grief often brings, all of which buttress our emotional healing.

Service shifts perspectives. After trauma or loss, we often get stuck in the *why*: Why did this happen? Why my child? There are no good answers. The act of serving others instead redirects us to create a new set of questions with important and powerful answers. It opens up *what* and *how* questions: What needs to change to make sure this never happens again? What has helped other families? How can I contribute to that future? The perspective shift helps us move from hopeless inaction to fulfilling change. Additionally, seeing the positive results of our efforts fosters gratitude.

Service transforms loss. When you serve others, finding some small positive outgrowth from a devastating tragedy, you may find that your tragedy transforms. It might become a powerful lesson for someone else, a new way of seeing the world, or a movement for positive change. You can find example after example of people who have taken their most devastating circumstances and transformed them into foundations, organizations, or global conversations. Two well-known examples are Candace Lightner, who founded Mothers Against Drunk Driving after a drunk driver killed her daughter, and John Walsh, creator of *America's Most Wanted*, who became a victims' rights activist after the murder of his son. But efforts need not be on such a large scale to make a difference—all it takes is a single act to begin to transform loss into purpose and positive change.

Nothing about trauma or grief is easy, and choosing to serve others while your own heart breaks demands incredible strength. But service reminds us that even in our deepest pain, we still have something to give. By sharing what we have lost, we create something that lives beyond us. For me, acts of service provide enormous fulfillment. I thank God for the Drews of this world and for those driven by profound love who step forward to make this world a better place. People who transform pain into acts of service often start critical conversations and enact cultural change.

We need our grievers. We need the ones we've lost and the ones who loved them to guide us toward a better way of being. So I ask you: What do you choose to do with that which you cannot change?

What Helped Me: Acts of Service

After Drew's death, I felt overwhelmed by helplessness, but focusing on service channeled my grief into something significant. If you're considering how service might help you, start by reflecting on the following questions—they may guide you toward a way to honor your loss while finding new meaning in your life:
- Your story has value. What would you like others to know or understand about your experience? What message do you want to share with the world?
- Even in the most painful loss, there's often an opportunity for positive impact. How can the experience you are grieving inspire change?
- Everyone has individual interests. What are your passions or skills? These might lead you to a cause or a way to serve that feels natural and fulfilling.
- Sometimes, the people or causes we connect with most deeply help us find our path forward. What causes or groups resonate with you?

Then, think about ways to act on your reflections. Service doesn't have to be grand or public; it can be small, personal, and intimate. Whether it is volunteering with a local nonprofit, raising awareness in your community, or sharing your story to inspire others, your service can help others while also healing you.

As you take the first steps, remember this is a process; small actions can lead to bigger ones. Start with something manageable and invite others along for support if it feels right. Every step you take is a step toward healing, a step toward transforming your grief into a legacy of love.

CHAPTER NINETEEN
EXPLORATION

Dear Drew,
I remember how you would marvel
at the stars at night and how it made me see the world
through your curiosity and wonder.
Love, Mom

WHILE AT FIRST my healing came in fits and bursts, over the years it built into a steady rhythm, thrumming with momentum toward a breakthrough. I reached a point where I felt fully ready to let go of the damaging aspects of my grief. I no longer needed pain and shame to feel connected to Drew. I yearned to grow my grief into something beautiful as I carried Drew with me, but I had very little idea how to do that.

Rather than feeling lost or discouraged, I looked to Drew for inspiration and made the conscious choice to approach this next phase of healing with a sense of childlike curiosity. Drew's eager and relentless "Why, Mommy?" echoed in my mind. I could see him so clearly, his little fingers wrapped around mine, his face scrunched in deep thought or eyes wide with the kind of wonder only children possess. "Why do stars twinkle, Mommy?" "Why does the wind make the trees dance?" "Why does the moon follow us?" His questions never stopped, and now they became my own. But instead of asking why grief had happened to me, I began asking: What now? What is possible beyond this pain? Drew's endless fascination with the world encouraged me to approach life with wonder and openness, turning even the smallest experiences into opportunities for discovery. What better way to carry his legacy forward than to look at the world as a giant playground?

I started with what already worked for me. Painting, writing, and energy work brought me real benefits, and these tools continued to bring me back to a place of grounded openness. I also knew that acts of service—big and small—would be important to me, but I felt there was something beyond talking about water safety that I was supposed to uncover. I also wanted a deeper understanding of my emotions, and I had unanswered questions of spirituality, so I allowed myself to explore. When questions about healing or grief arose, I carved out time to research them. I didn't settle for pat answers; I stopped only when I found an answer that worked for *me*. Once I found answers, I didn't keep them to myself. I got braver about starting conversations around grief—the ones most people shied away from—because every time I shared honestly about my experience, I could feel the pain lifting. I let curiosity take me to a place of possibility, and I allowed myself to start dreaming about the future again.

Most importantly, I stayed focused on my connection to Drew, and he began to lead me places. One afternoon, I sat with my journal, flipping through old entries—most filled with grief, anger, and longing. Then I found something unexpected: an entry from

CHAPTER 19: EXPLORATION

before the accident. It was a list of things Drew had taught me: "To laugh loudly." "To chase butterflies." "To see shapes in the clouds." "To believe in magic." My breath caught in my throat. These were his lessons, and I had forgotten them. That was the moment I knew I needed to write not just for myself but for him and for anyone who might need to remember that joy and grief can coexist. I felt compelled to tell my story from the beginning, and it poured out of me. When the download stopped, I decided to publish *Lessons from Neverland*, a memoir that covered my childhood, losing Drew, and more. I viewed it as a cathartic personal project; putting it out into the world felt validating, but I did not expect the response it got.

Lessons from Neverland touched people in a way that encouraged them to reach out to me. Some contacted me personally; others wanted to arrange interviews and speaking engagements. This time, instead of speaking about water safety, people asked me to talk about my journey through grief. As a result of those requests, I realized I could contribute by showing up as myself and speaking openly. Though I didn't intend it when I put pen to paper, I found my book connected me to a community of bereaved parents.

People started asking me for help. Unfortunately, more parents in Yuma had lost children to drowning than I had realized. Because I spoke about water safety in a public role, people thought I had the answers. I didn't, but I could at least share what worked for me. When the first mother who had lost her child to drowning reached out to me and confided softly, "I don't know how to survive this," my heart clenched because I knew that feeling too well. I didn't have the perfect words or a solution to erase her pain, but I knew how to sit with her in it. "You don't have to survive it all at once," I told her. "Just take one breath, one step, one moment at a time." I offered people my raw vulnerability, I witnessed their grief for as long as they needed, and I helped them take action toward healing when they were ready. Later, some of those parents would update me on their progress, which assured me I had something worth sharing. I found my way forward by helping others find theirs.

I felt like I had backed my way out of hell, step-by-step, until one day I looked up and realized I stood closer to heaven, closer to Drew. Each step was marked by realizations that brought light into the darkness: understanding that my grief didn't define me, discovering that helping others could heal my own wounds, and recognizing that Drew's love was still alive in every moment I chose to live fully. These realizations were like stars breaking through the night sky, guiding me forward. I could hear him whisper in my ear, in that raspy little child's voice that sounded like he smoked a pack a day: "Isn't this so fun, Mommy? Now what?" For the first time in a long time, I whispered back: "I don't know yet, but I can't wait to find out."

Though I trusted Drew to lead me—and I had started to trust myself again—I certainly didn't navigate each step perfectly. When speaking, sometimes I lost the audience, and my message simply didn't land. I made mistakes and ran into roadblocks, but I got creative, and I didn't limit myself to obvious solutions. I tried new things, pushing myself into areas I never anticipated. I accepted invitations to speak about overcoming grief, sadness, and trauma well before I felt qualified to do so. One speaking engagement led to the next, and before I knew it, I was traveling around the world. From bereaved parents seeking to transform pain into purpose to tech experts at Google exploring adversity's role in leadership, I spoke to whoever would listen to me talk about the wisdom Drew had imparted.

Eventually, a friend of mine came to me with another bold idea: start a TV show that confronts tough topics with a positive outlook.

It sounded right up my alley. We called it *The Ripple Effect* to signify the meaningful and wide-reaching impact of one positive action. Drew's accident was the stone thrown in the pond, and the ripples continued to expand before my eyes.

I didn't know exactly what the future would look like, but the more I maintained my curiosity about the uncertain aspects of my life, the more peace I seemed to have. So I kept chasing the unpredictable to see where it would lead. And each time I explored a new idea, took a chance, or did something I believed would make the world a better place, I could hear Drew cheering me on: "Isn't this so fun, Mommy?"

Grief is a beautiful invitation to explore, expand, and transform.

Most people think grief should be avoided or quickly resolved. It is often framed as an unwelcome, negative force of life that steals our ability to function and thrive. Cultural narratives deepen the perception, casting grief as a problem to be fixed rather than a natural occurrence to explore. While grief certainly destabilizes us, I believe we have more choice in what we do with it than our culture tends to acknowledge. Grief, though painful, need not be a limitation. It can serve as an entry point to greater self-awareness, resilience, and creativity. It can be an invitation to grow, connect, and create a life that acknowledges both the pain of loss and the possibilities that emerge from it. By recasting grief as a teacher and engaging with it fully, suffering can become a source of strength and inspiration. We can choose to see the beautiful aspects of our grief.

In both personal and larger societal conversations, many people are scared to suggest that something positive can come from grief. Initially, it can feel like an insult to the memory of our lost loved one or a dismissal of our trauma. But considering the possibility of "more" stretches our capacity for compassion, understanding, and resilience. It expands our minds to see and feel new perspectives, and along the way, it can open us to positive experiences we've never contemplated, many of which can pay tribute to those we miss, creating connection in absence.

Grief has the capacity to teach lessons that cannot be learned through joy or ease. It reveals the depth of our emotional landscape, highlights the fragility and preciousness of life, and forces us to confront our values and priorities. Healing, in many ways, is like mining for gems in the depths of the earth. The process is laborious and the environment dark, but with patience and perseverance, we can uncover treasures—moments of clarity, connection, and growth—that shine brilliantly against the backdrop of our pain. Each new discovery, like a gem, becomes a piece of the life we build moving forward.

We can choose to believe grief has the potential to offer us more than sadness, and with that choice, we can invite and nurture the unique gifts that come from navigating it. Grief can be a season of life that births new creativity and discovery, once we are ready to see it that way. When warmly embraced, grief can transform us and lead to a life larger than the pain it brings. In the liminal space between loss and new beginnings, we can start to imagine possibilities. We can begin to ask: Who am I now? We don't need all the answers; the act of exploration itself heals us.

What helped me most in exploring grief wasn't trying to escape it or find some quick solution; it was leaning into it, even when it felt unbearable. Grief forced me to slow down, sit with my emotions, and ask questions I'd never considered: What does this pain have to teach me? What lies beneath the surface of my sadness? What parts of myself or my life are waiting to be uncovered in this space of loss?

Grief, when approached with curiosity rather than resistance, opens us up to profound moments of presence. It teaches us to pay attention, to explore the depths of our emotions, and to see the hidden gems waiting to be mined. These discoveries do not happen overnight. They come in moments of stillness, in the willingness to ask questions, and in the courage to try new things even though we don't feel ready.

You already know the healing process isn't linear; I also want you to know it doesn't have to be so serious and arduous. Curiosity, and even playfulness, can become a mindset, a lens we use to see new possibilities, invite ease, and be present. Curiosity invites us to question what healing means for us personally. It encourages us to explore creative outlets, spiritual practices, and forms of connection that resonate with us—even if they don't fit into the traditional idea of grief and healing. The process of staying curious often means thinking beyond what's expected or "normal." Instead of asking, "What should I do next?," curiosity asks, "What feels meaningful to me?" It might prompt us to follow an unconventional calling or pursue a dream that once seemed unattainable, but above all, curiosity asks us to embrace the unknown. Curiosity reminds us that it's okay to try, fail, and try again—as long as we keep searching for what feels right. It invites us to honor our past while dreaming, exploring, and creating space for something new to emerge.

Transformation takes time, and the beauty of exploration is that it's messy and experimental. There's no pressure to arrive at a defined purpose or clear vision yet. If you feel overwhelmed by the idea of transformation, remember this: Healing doesn't have to be big or dramatic to be meaningful. It can happen in the quiet moments, in the small acts of care you offer yourself, and in the simple decision to keep moving forward. Practice self-compassion, release perfectionism, and trust the unfolding process.

When navigating the search for meaning and direction, tune out the world and listen to your heart. After enduring the hardest days of grief or trauma, you are capable of more than you think. Trusting yourself is the key to finding your unique voice and dreams. Notice what feels true now—not for who you were before your loss, but for who you are becoming after it—and keep exploring.

What Helped Me: Exploring Grief's Gifts

Exploring grief gave me many discoveries and gifts, and it made me feel *good*. This idea of being curious in grief might feel foreign to you, which is a natural response in our culture. Take some time to reflect on what grief might offer if you allow yourself to explore it.

Choose a quiet space where you won't be interrupted. Close your eyes, take a few deep breaths, and ask yourself:
- What am I feeling in this moment?
- What is this grief trying to tell me?
- What would curiosity lead me to try?

Write down whatever comes to mind, even if it feels messy or unclear. Exploration doesn't require certainty, only openness. Even in grief, we can remain curious about what is possible, what we might learn, and how we might grow.

CHAPTER TWENTY
SPIRITUALITY

Dear Drew,
I find comfort in the moments of stillness,
where I can reflect on our love.
Love, Mom

FROM AN EARLY AGE, my relationship with God felt precarious. Raised in a conservative Christian church, I learned that I must follow his word precisely to be invited into the celestial kingdom. God's love felt conditional, an all-or-nothing exchange that too often seemed punishing. Years later, when Joey and I married, we shared a Christian faith, but we didn't share the same denominational upbringing. After my childhood introduction to religion, I was fine never stepping foot in a church again, so we decided not to raise our kids in a specific religion. But Drew had other plans.

Around age four, Drew started asking me about God. He loved the movie *The Prince of Egypt*, an animated retelling of the Book of Exodus, and his friends from preschool would talk about the activities they did at church. Once his questions started, they never slowed down: "Why did God make me?" "Can he hear me when I pray?" "Where does he live?" To satisfy Drew's curiosity, we took him to churches of different denominations; he visited friends' churches; we read books. And he loved all of it. He loved God, and I rarely knew what to do with that.

One day, as I prepared dinner, Drew walked right up to me, took my hand, and pressed it against his heart. "God told me we live here forever." Then he raised his tiny hand and placed his palm flat against my heart. "Mommy, I will always be right here. I will always be with you." Before I could respond, he went back to playing with his Tonka trucks, zooming around the house in joy. *Where does this kid get this stuff? He must have heard it from someone.* But I never could pinpoint the moment he learned that eternal truth. He connected to the spiritual world in a way that most of us miss, and in his short life, he managed to reintroduce us to God before we needed our faith most.

However, after Drew's accident, I turned my back on God for a while. If he could take away my most precious gift at any moment, then he was not a God I trusted. Even through my anger, though, I never stopped talking to him. Driving in the car, I'd shout, "I'm not okay, God! Do you hear me? Hello?! What the hell were you thinking? This is too much!" Other days I'd curl in a ball under my blankets and think, *How could you do this to me?* In the moments I mustered the courage to pray, it was never hands folded, eyes closed, head bowed. It didn't feel reverent. I had to get real with God. We went on like this for years—although God didn't usually say much—until he sent me a guide.

I met the Reverend Kevin Ross when I interviewed him for my TV show, *The Ripple Effect*. He talked about how his relationship with God helped him show up as a force for good in this world, and

I realized that I wanted that too. After filming, we talked for a while, and I asked him to be my spiritual mentor. Kevin cautioned me that living a spiritual life would require action. I would need to learn specific things to change my outlook and live from a higher awareness. Prayer and other spiritual practices would help me build my faith, find inner peace, create a sense of safety, and connect to my innate divine wisdom. He said, "No matter what is happening in your life—whether there is chaos and confusion, pain and worry, illness or death—God offers you strength, courage, and comfort."

I decided I was ready. I was curious to start exploring my relationship with God again, like Drew had been curious all those years ago, so "Rev. Kev" and I dove right in. After I finished telling him about Drew's accident and everything that followed, I'll never forget what he said: "You have no idea what a blessed woman you are."

I couldn't pretend to be anything but confused. "What do you mean I'm blessed?" All my life I had felt cursed: My mother battled cancer. My son drowned. My husband cheated. I lived in anticipation of the next shoe dropping.

But, Kevin posited, what if these adversities allowed me to draw closer to God in ways I could not have without them? If struggle was divinely intended to bring me closer to God, to fortify my spirit for what lay ahead, then I was receiving blessings, not curses.

I had another choice to make: allow my struggles to turn my relationship with God into a space of resentment and disconnection, or work to grow my relationship with God inside the struggle.

Then Kevin said something that felt even crazier: "You are the bright idea of your creator. He created you as his gift to this world, and he delights in you."

For so many years, I had questioned whether Drew's loss was divine punishment, if God had given me that pain because I was truly unlovable or undeserving of his grace. Though I had already moved beyond the belief that my experiences were punishments, the suggestion to see them as acts of faith that provided the growth and healing I needed left me astonished.

Then Kevin directed my gaze toward a small piece of pottery that looked like it had been broken and reconstructed, its repairs lined with gold. "Kintsugi," he said. "A traditional Japanese art form. When the broken pieces are lacquered together, it makes something stronger, and in highlighting the seams with gold powder, it makes something beautiful. The technique takes years to master."

As I traced my fingertips across each crack, I could suddenly see it: Spirituality is that beautiful gold powder. God brings me back to wholeness. I am not meant to sit on a shelf untouched. When we break into pieces from use and love, as we inevitably do, we must believe in the beauty of putting ourselves back together.

God's role in my life became unmistakable. I stopped seeing myself as broken and started tapping into an untouched part of myself. That pot became my visual representation that God is always there for me. I am loved. I am worthy. The evidence is all around me and within me. I simply had to choose to see it.

It brought tears to my eyes. The life I had desired was more than a mere hope. There was a new possibility for the healing that could take place in my heart. I was the unique expression of my creator. And now, from a mess of shards and fragments, I saw new potential.

When we feel broken, spirituality can help us become whole again.

When we are grieving, it is easy to feel untethered, to question everything we once believed. It is hard to have faith in any destiny or higher power that gives us loss. It is normal to reel for a while, to writhe against the constraints of our past spiritual understanding. The quest to rediscover spirituality after loss will ask you to dig deeper, to question and search and expand your relationship. But the goal is not to find all the answers; it is to lean into faith, sitting with the discomfort and trusting the process of being made whole again.

Before I continue, let me first say that I am not a theologian. For some of you, my observations will seem elementary. For others, they may open up new possibilities. But to be clear, I am not trying to convert anyone to a particular religion.

I believe that spirituality is personal. Some people find comfort and belonging in a formal religion while others prefer the more intuitive spiritual experiences found in nature. However, because I grew up Christian, that is the path and language I am most familiar with, so I use the name "God" for what one might call "the divine." Please substitute your own language—a higher power, Source, the universe, the One. If you are not religious, or even what you think of as spiritual, think of "god" as your inner power or your higher self. Author Julia Cameron (*The Artist's Way*) suggests thinking of GOD as "good orderly direction."

My point is: Don't let my personal language trip you up or stop you from receiving the broader message. I invite you to explore spiritual practice even if you don't follow a particular religion or believe in a deity; the practice itself can still make a difference.

The Spiritual Relationship

Spirituality doesn't just happen; it is a relationship we cultivate. Nearly every spiritual tradition contains rituals for regular prayer, meditation, or similar acts. The Catholics have specific times for prayer, such as lauds (morning prayer) and vespers (evening prayer).

In Islam, the faithful are called to salah (prayer) five times a day. Buddhists also have regular prayer, chanting, and meditation practices that have a similar intent of fostering connection and focus. But spiritual practice need not involve pious prayer or meditation. It can also involve a quiet thought or yogic chant, a wish upon a star or a walk in the forest. It can include incense or drums or icons. And an individual's spiritual practice can encompass numerous traditions.

Regular spiritual practice not only deepens our relationship with God but also expands our capacity to receive whatever God can offer. In my experience, the divine offers strength and wisdom beyond what we can access alone. Just as writing regularly makes the words flow more easily, maintaining a regular spiritual practice strengthens our connection to the divine so that we can access it more readily.

When life unfolds in ways we don't want or understand, we have the unique opportunity to turn to God. The Reverend Robert Brumet, a Unity minister, writes, "The first step in spiritual healing is to recognize our own needs for healing." He goes on to say, "Spiritual healing begins as we turn to God for help. We turn to God because our original nature is spiritual. As spiritual beings, we are expressions of God, never separated from our Source."

The strength of God is within us to help us persevere through hard times. Sometimes simply knowing that God is with us can help us show up differently. When the flow of life is challenging, through faith we find resources for resilience.

Spiritual Surrender

When I enter the spiritual side of myself, I can receive wisdom and awareness that I do not have access to in my humanness. What is possible through God is now possible for me. To access divine wisdom, comfort, and assistance, sometimes we can ask, and it is immediately there. Sometimes we must surrender. Spiritual surrender is an acknowledgment that we have reached our human limitations and need support beyond our capabilities. Surrender may include admitting our own failure, fragility, or lack. When we surrender, we invite God (the divine, the universe, Source) to step in. Surrender is not meekness; it is not collapse; it is not giving up. It is acknowledging that which is, and asking for help.

But surrender is not passive. We don't merely put the problem in God's hands and then resign ourselves to waiting. There is no magic. God doesn't—*presto!*—solve all our problems. The act of surrender opens us to new wisdom and possibilities, but we must still take action. Faith is an *active* practice. It requires an engaged relationship with God, even when that means asking him (her, it, them) to take the lead.

Sometimes we have to ask our higher power to sit with us through discomfort or guide us through blind turns. More often, faith calls us to participate by trusting it. Sometimes our role is to be still, to not worry about the *how* or the *when*. Those might not be for us to know yet. And that's part of what makes faith uncomfortable: the uncertainty. For me, when I don't know how things will unfold, I trust God by acting in grateful anticipation as though I already believe what is needed will be done.

However, I will be the first to admit that I often struggle with turning things over to God. I can say the words "God, give me the presence of mind and the spirit of love to move through this; help me see what I'm not seeing," but I still have a hard time getting out of my own way. In my humanness, I still think I can make the difference on my own. That's when I know I have to surrender more.

It also takes practice to discern true guidance from the ego's agenda. We think the answer should look a certain way, but God doesn't do things the way we do. Instead, we must get curious: *I wonder how this will all resolve?*

There is no magic in surrender and faith, yet they are infinitely magical. The insights gained—what Buddhism might call enlightenment—can drastically change the trajectory of our healing. When we are supported by spirituality, healing needn't follow traditional timelines.

Finding Wholeness

Our spirituality can grow exponentially in times of struggle. Adversity and trauma aren't spiritual punishments; they are tough realities that can either splinter or strengthen our spiritual relationship. Through struggle, we can appreciate peace and happiness. We know light to the degree we know dark; in darkness, we are invited to draw closer to God. When we trust the unconditional love of God (the universe, a higher power, the One), we can look at a scatter of broken pieces and see the beauty that remains. Faith fills the cracks with love, mending us when life feels most fragile. Spirituality leads us to wholeness, our possibility never diminished.

In my faith, I believe God created us with a divine imprint. We are always who he (she, it, they) created us to be. In other paths, the language may vary—we are a manifestation of God, we carry the spark of the divine in us—but that divinity is always there, regardless of our loss, trauma, and heartbreak. Our circumstances can become difficult, but who we innately are never changes. You are divine. I am divine. We are divine. So, in a sense, we were never really broken; we were just waiting for faith to fill us with love in all the fractured places.

Spirituality invites us to embrace a limitless potential that extends far beyond the boundaries of our human abilities. It offers a conduit between what we can manage on our own and the expansive strength that faith provides. I have absolute faith that everything unfolding for me is designed to be used for my highest and best purpose. But to achieve that, I know I must accept, welcome, and surrender to each experience. When we surrender in moments of limitation, we create space for something larger to step in and fortify us. In that partnership, we discover that what once felt impossible becomes achievable, and the boundaries we thought defined us no longer apply.

Through faith, we are not just whole—we are truly limitless.

What Helped Me: Affirmative Prayer

When many people think of prayer, they think of asking God for something. Affirmative prayer, which I use regularly, takes a different approach. While affirmative prayer can connect with God, it is more about creating internal alignment (so if you are not religious, please don't let the word *prayer* deter you).

An affirmative prayer makes an intentional, positive statement about a desired outcome and is rooted in the belief that this outcome already exists or is fully attainable. For instance, instead of saying, "God, please help me find peace," an affirmative prayer might declare, "I am at peace now; I know that peace is my natural state." Rather than saying, "God, please help me find a new job," an affirmative prayer might state, "I know I am guided to the right job."

Words and thoughts wield creative power. You have surely felt this: the colleague who needs a new job yet constantly complains about the search process, or the friend who seeks love but bad-mouths every first date. You can feel their negative energy, so it is no surprise they struggle to find interested employers or partners. Our words and thoughts shape our energy, aligning us with the outcomes they create (remember the Map of Consciousness from Chapter 9?).

Affirmative prayer emphasizes the belief that we are each being led to our highest good, despite how things might appear at the moment. Once we make an affirmative prayer, we must trust the process (God, the universe, Source) and listen to the internal guidance we receive. This process empowers us to visualize the future with full faith that it is both possible and real. Through affirmative prayer, we cocreate with the universe by giving thanks in advance for the goodness we bring to life.

I invite you to try affirmative prayer using these basic steps:
1. Take a moment to center yourself with a breathing or grounding exercise.
2. Feel your connection to God or the universe. You might say "I honor my connection to the divine" or "I feel my connection to the universe."
3. Declare your intention: "I affirm that the right job exists, one that uses my skills and talents, and I am confidently moving along the right path toward it."
4. Express gratitude for the anticipated outcome: "I am grateful for the gifts I can offer the world and the opportunities that are unfolding for me."
5. Release the prayer: "I release this prayer, knowing it is already done."

Affirmative prayer is not about pleading or bargaining; it is about declaring, with faith, that even in grief and uncertainty, love and divine support remain.

CHAPTER TWENTY-ONE
PURPOSE

Dear Drew,
I am discovering that it's possible
to find joy and purpose again while
carrying you in my heart.
Love, Mom

ABOUT FIFTEEN YEARS after Drew's accident, a friend reached out to me for support after he and his wife lost one of their younger children to a drowning accident in their backyard swimming pool. He asked if I would come meet with them and the rest of their kids. Though we had known one another since high school, we had drifted apart over the years, so I didn't know how a conversation with them would unfold.

When I went to their house, I took a picture quilt a friend had sewn from all my favorite images of Drew and me. As I sat with the family and listened to their story, their faces reflected gratitude and relief to finally speak their hearts and trust that someone understood. Surprisingly, I found I made the most difference with the children. They touched the quilt and asked questions as I described the photos: "This is Drew playing with his favorite toy." "Here we are on the beach." As we talked, the younger children would bring me their sister's toys or pictures of her and say, "This toy was her favorite," or "I like to sleep in her pajamas." They loved sharing how they still connected with the sister they had lost.

For the first time, I realized that sharing my story offered not only a point of deep connection and shared heartbreak but also a space of collective hope and optimism. In that moment, I knew I was standing in the space that Theresa had once held for me, passing on the same kindness that I had once received. I felt an enormous sense of appreciation for everything that Theresa's letter meant to me and everything it had enabled me to become. Rev. Kev was right: I was blessed.

When I left my friend's house that day, I started recognizing my potential as an advocate for grievers, and more importantly, I started to see it as a life purpose. In the span of a couple of hours, this one experience had both broadened and narrowed the focus of what I wanted my life to become. I was already making space for others to grieve and heal by sharing my experiences, but I wanted to pair my personal testimony with the knowledge of grief counseling and trauma support, which would require education. After research and some hints from Drew, I enrolled in two different coaching programs, one through the International Coach Federation as well as a specialized program that called to me, the Heart-Centered Life Coaching program by Robin Johnson. When I added the knowledge and practices from these programs to the years of study I had invested in my own healing, I felt more confident and capable of pursuing my calling with vigor. The further I followed this road, the clearer it became: My purpose was to pursue writing and coaching with an emphasis on supporting people who were ready to move forward in connection with their departed loved one. I had yearned for that connection myself, and it was exactly what I wanted to help others discover.

I believe that everything in my life has a cumulative purpose. All those painful moments, and the time I spent learning from them, could add up to something greater—if I chose to make a difference. At this point, my life grew bigger than my grief. My purpose gave me a pathway forward that I could embrace without feelings of guilt or shame. The life I had once envisioned for myself and my family had been shattered by Drew's accident, but I had worked hard to put the pieces back together. Now, as I looked ahead, I could see what was left: an unfinished mosaic that still held all the promise of a beautiful life.

Purpose is created, not found.

At a basic level, a purpose is a goal, an aim, an objective to be attained. But here I am speaking of a deeper purpose, a life purpose. You might say it is the thing that you are on this earth to do, or the thing you want to dedicate yourself to.

Purpose is not something we stumble upon in the dark corners of our grief. It is a light we kindle by taking deliberate actions to transform pain into meaning. Purpose reshapes pain into a resource for growth. It shifts the focus from "Why did this happen?" to "What can I build from here?" While the ache of loss may never fully disappear, purpose offers a way to integrate it into our lives, fostering connection, hope, and resilience. When we connect our actions to something larger than ourselves, we find clarity and comfort as the loss begins to feel meaningful rather than arbitrary.

Our purpose emerges from intentional reflection, small actions, and the courage to grow. It is cumulative, so everything we've talked about in this book so far, and especially in the past few chapters, builds to support the idea of creating purpose. There is a moment when you accept that who you *were* is no longer who you *are*. Purpose allows you to simultaneously respect the past and celebrate the future without feeling guilty.

To be perfectly clear, when I noticed the nudge of purpose while talking with my friend's family, it did not come out of the blue. I had already been taking regular small steps in that direction: self-care and personal healing work initially, speaking about water safety and then grief, writing a book, hosting a TV show. While I was generally headed in the right direction, the road meandered. For instance, when I launched my TV show, *The Ripple Effect*, I thought I had found my purpose, but soon businesspeople, sponsors, and the push to monetize everything turned the whole enterprise into *work*. I didn't need more work; I needed purpose, so I moved on.

In retrospect, I *had* found my purpose (or at least *a* purpose), but I did not yet know how to shape or cultivate it. This is a normal occurrence; you might experience it too. Eventually I reframed my thinking about purpose from having a career to engaging with a community. I needed a place to share and serve.

This leads me to a key point: Purpose is not static; it evolves as you grow. Creating your purpose is not an overnight effort or a six-month effort or a yearlong effort. It took me almost two decades. And you don't realize how far you have come until you look back and you see the distance you've traveled. Microsteps still move you forward.

For me, the purpose now feels like a collaboration with Drew. Because of what I have been through, I can act as a credible witness, an empathetic listener. I can recognize potential where others cannot. When people who are grieving feel lost, I see that they are actually weeding through the physical, mental, and emotional things they no longer need. My purpose has provided meaning. It has created something that will last beyond my time here, which is important to me. In my work, I honor Drew's brief life and the tremendous impact it has had on the community, but my purpose is also about the legacy I want *my* life to have.

Your purpose will look and feel different from mine. My purpose would not fit you; your purpose would not fit me. You must craft your own purpose through taking the needed steps. I know someone who writes poetry, with the purpose of expressing the inexpressible so people feel seen. One family I know has a purpose of making others feel loved, especially those who are often marginalized; they bring that purpose to life through random acts of kindness, like anonymously paying for someone's groceries. Another family created a rodeo that benefits hospice to fulfill their purpose of comforting people at the end of life. All these beneficial efforts originated in loss. You must explore that place where fulfillment and meaning meet service so you can do what feels right and authentic for you.

Purpose is a magical thing. When you experience it, you know it. When you are aligned to it, you know it. Once you create it, it's undeniable. It adds focus where there was once ambiguity and lets you conceive of a future that is not imposed upon you but chosen with conviction. However, purpose is not an abstract concept; it is something we live daily. Every decision, every interaction, every moment of service contributes to our evolving sense of purpose. By actively engaging in meaningful work, even in small ways, we strengthen the foundation of our new life.

To truly integrate purpose into our lives, we must understand that it is both an internal process and an external process. Internally, it requires reflection, understanding our pain, and redefining our identity in the wake of loss. Externally, it demands action, service, and the courage to step beyond our comfort zones. Through intentional steps, we turn our pain into power. When we practice purpose regularly, it becomes a sustaining force, allowing us to move forward with clarity and strength. When we view it as a living, breathing part of our lives, we embrace its potential to continually shape and enrich our experiences. By making space for purpose in our daily routines, we ensure that meaning, healing, and joy remain at the center of our journey.

What Helped Me: The P.U.R.P.O.S.E. Framework

In hindsight, I realized that the intuitive steps I took throughout my healing process were leading me into a life of purpose. I later formalized these steps into the P.U.R.P.O.S.E. framework. As you move toward creating your purpose, you may find it useful as an overarching concept and as a periodic reflection exercise.

P: Pause and reflect. Reflection helps you uncover what matters most, offering a compass to guide your actions. Ask yourself: What values do I want to live by now? What lessons have I learned from my loss?

U: Understand triggers and strengths. Identify what challenges lie ahead and what resources you already have at hand. Ask yourself: What strengthens me during tough times?

R: Reach out for support. Consider connecting with a trusted friend, therapist, or support group. Ask yourself: Is there someone I trust to share my journey with?

P: Pursue small steps daily. Purpose doesn't require grand gestures. It begins with small, meaningful steps. Example: Dedicate ten minutes a day to a meaningful project. Revisit a passion or hobby you set aside during your grief.

O: Open yourself to joy. Find and cherish small moments of happiness. Example: Spend time daily doing something that brings you peace or that uplifts you.

S: Set boundaries. Protect your energy by saying no to things that drain you. Ask yourself: What relationships or habits can I adjust to support my healing?

E: Embrace growth. Accept that growth does not have an endpoint; it is ongoing. Ask yourself: What have I learned, and how can I use it to move forward?

By consciously creating purpose, you recognize your loss while building a future filled with resilience, connection, and joy. Remember: Your purpose is not out there waiting to be found. It is within you, waiting to be created.

CHAPTER TWENTY-TWO
VISION

Dear Drew,
I often talk to you,
sharing my thoughts and dreams
as if you were here.
Love, Mom

CREATING MY PURPOSE in life was just the starting point. I didn't automatically know how take action toward implementing it. How could I best advocate for people who were navigating loss? What did that look like? How would I move forward in that capacity? I needed a clear picture of what I was trying to build.

It took me time and energy to develop a vision that matched my purpose. I paused much of my speaking work in order to refocus, design my next destination, and begin defining the steps to reach it. As it happens, I've had a lot of practice creating new visions for myself, beginning with Drew's accident. Without my permission, loss erased the life I once pictured. It forced me to confront a reality that no longer aligned with my expectations, and I had to reimagine my future in ways I never wanted to consider.

At first, my vision wasn't bold or far-reaching—it was the flicker of hope sparked by a letter from a stranger. I could scarcely imagine a life without Drew. I survived minute to minute, and picturing anything more seemed cruel if not impossible. Though I had no sense of a vision for my future, I knew what I wanted to feel: less pain, a momentary escape, some kind of connection to Drew's memory. Those feelings became my trail markers; if I could get from one to the next, I was heading in the right direction.

As I began to heal, I noticed tiny glimmers of clarity breaking through the fog and hinting at the possibility of something beyond the pain: the kindness of a stranger, the way sunlight caught Drew's favorite flower, or the stillness of a deep breath that didn't feel heavy. These small experiences created the space I needed to pause and reflect, if only for a moment. I found myself asking tentative questions: What could life look like if it didn't hurt so much? Could I honor Drew while still finding peace for myself? These weren't the bold, life-altering visions that would come later, but they marked the beginning of something important—the willingness to wonder.

When it came time to do the deeper healing work, I needed a stronger image to hold onto. I remember slipping into a lucid dream—that strange dream state in which you know you are dreaming—where I was Joan of Arc. I sat on the back of a glorious white horse. I wore a shiny suit of armor and a helmet, my hair somehow still blowing in the wind. In one hand I clutched my bedazzled shield—because I do love my bling—and in the other I raised my sword. The scene was surreal yet intensely purposeful, as though my subconscious had sent me a lifeline. As I looked at the battlefield before me,

CHAPTER 22: VISION

I let out a cry: "Bring it on! I'm ready for the challenge! This will not destroy me! Bring! It! On!" I was not just fighting to survive grief; I was preparing to battle for my future. I needed to challenge a lifetime of deeply held narratives. While Joan fought soldiers, I swung my sword at my own thoughts and self-perpetuated unhealthy dynamics, engaging my inner turmoil and gradually inching closer to becoming my ideal self. Whenever I started to waver in my conviction, I returned to Joan like my North Star guiding me to victory.

As my healing journey continued, my vision changed based on what I needed in each stage. When I started exploring alternative healing practices, I became Queen Elizabeth I, an unconventional ruler who never married and whose vision established the foundation of the modern Church of England. I saw myself as an "out there" healer who did things most people would roll their eyes at, but I knew that deeper healing awaited me outside the mainstream approach to grief. This defiance felt both frightening and liberating, an audacious declaration of self-belief.

As I held onto the changes these visions sparked in my life, my capabilities expanded. I began imagining a life that felt steady—even peaceful. The idea of thriving rather than surviving took shape. Gradually, my visions evolved from embodying emblematic leaders to seeing myself in snapshots of an ideal future: laughing with Devin and Hope in front of the Christmas tree, sitting next to Joey as we cheered the kids across the stage at graduation. My dreams felt impossibly far away at times, but they gave me something to aim for. These glimpses of hope reminded me that joy and connection were still within reach.

Over more than two decades, my vision transformed from survival to growth, and eventually to impact. Writing blogs, sharing my story onstage, and working with grieving clients weren't parts of my original vision because I *couldn't* have imagined them at the start. But as my capability and capacity for healing grew, so did my dreams.

Today my vision is bigger than ever. It has expanded from my personal healing to the mark I want to make on the world. What once guided my desperate search for survival has become a road map for my purpose. I am dedicated to supporting grievers through writing, resources, and coaching, and I'm looking ahead to what's next: a nonprofit organization dedicated to providing water safety education and resources on a national level. I can envision scholarships and support for siblings who have experienced loss and an entire community of support for parents who have lost children to drowning accidents. While I never could have seen that in the days or months after Drew passed, now it is the only thing I can see when I picture the life ahead of me.

Our vision for the future evolves as we do.

Vision is our picture of what the future could look like. Having a purpose without a vision is like setting out on a journey without a clear destination or a map—we often end up lost or stuck in our good intentions. A vision provides a sense of direction and guides decisions, actions, and priorities. In business, a vision often aims to inspire employees to achieve the company's long-term goals. An entertainment company might envision a future where "storytelling fosters understanding and connection across cultures." An educational institution might picture an environment where "knowledge knows no barriers, and every person has the opportunity to learn and thrive." For individuals, a vision may entail specific goals and guide personal development efforts. A runner envisions crossing the finish line of a marathon, and that vision guides them to embrace the discipline and resilience needed to train for the race. Whether for a business, an individual, or a family, a vision embodies the values and aspirations we have and the impact we hope to create.

Grief forces us to rebuild our future from the ground up, so in a healing context, vision can seem tenuous at times. However, I have found that having a clear vision—whether simple or far-reaching—aids in the healing process because it provides an anchor to hold onto during uncertainty and a lodestar to follow when the path seems unclear. The presence of loss does not negate the ability to dream; rather, it deepens our understanding of why our dreams matter. And as with purpose, vision is not something we stumble upon; it is something we craft with intention.

When imagining life after loss, we tend to start small. We can't let our hopes and dreams get too big, because the possibility of disappointment feels threatening, like it might destroy all our progress in one blow. But regardless of where it starts, your vision will grow with you, reflecting your progress in each step. What once felt like an impossible leap becomes an achievable milestone and, eventually, a transformative accomplishment.

When you are newly grieving, the idea of envisioning a future may be inconceivable. However, even if you can't articulate a specific vision like "I want to start a nonprofit," in my experience, most people can still identify an emotion they want to feel: "I want to be at peace," "I want to experience joy," "I want to feel like I am giving back to the world." These emotions become the seeds of a vision, maybe in snapshots initially: making it through a meal with family, taking a walk, spending a day without tears. These small victories lead to larger pictures: a peaceful afternoon reading a book or a meaningful conversation with a friend.

Eventually, desires for the future grow beyond snapshots. You start to see versions of the person you want to become, plans for the life you want to build, and goals you want to accomplish. Your vision may have everything to do with your loss, or it may have nothing to do with it. But as it takes shape and grows, you will come to realize that your boldest vision is still entirely within reach. Even as your vision expands, grief will still walk beside you. A vision does not require you to "move on"; it asks only that you keep moving forward.

When you heal enough to begin crafting a somewhat more expansive vision, especially for implementing the purpose you have created, I encourage you to do it thoughtfully and focus on your inner voice, paying special attention to what your heart says. The goal is not to craft a flawless or unrealistic picture of your life; it is to discover what matters most and capture it.

In his book *On Writing: A Memoir of the Craft*, bestselling author Stephen King describes how he writes his books "with the door closed" and revises them "with the door open." Meant to be taken figuratively, King's approach means he mentally closes the door to others' feedback while he generates ideas and drafts; he writes for himself. Then, when it is time for revision and editing, he opens himself up to suggestions. But he makes sure he captures his own ideas before he lets someone else influence his words.

When you envision a new future for yourself, start by dreaming with the door closed. Create a private space—mentally and physically if needed—to figure out what your heart and mind have to say. Don't edit or judge your thoughts because this is not the final draft. Instead, focus on listening and accepting what comes up for you and capturing the details. If grief has taken away your sense of self, this exercise is an opportunity to reclaim it.

Once you have expressed your ideas and begun crafting a picture, you can open the door up to ask for support and feedback. But choose your support system carefully. If you are going to open up about your deepest desires, you need to trust that the person receiving them will treat them with compassion, respect, and encouragement. I suggest sticking to your "with-you-for-you" people (see Chapter 11).

When you do share your vision, it may help to set some parameters. If parts of your vision are nonnegotiable, make sure everyone understands what's open for discussion and what's not. Then listen. Let your heart consider the feedback you receive and try to resist allowing the mind to take over. You can always "close the door" again if needed. Feel free to shut out doubt, especially if someone else doubts your abilities, and consider closing the door when people start looking at *your* vision through the lens of *their* life. Your vision is your own; it does not need to be understood by others to be worthy of pursuit.

At some point, you must close the door again and solidify your vision; otherwise, the weight of others' opinions might paralyze you. But remember that your vision evolves as you do, so nothing is set in stone. The important part is that your vision reflects your values, your healing, and your hope. What do you think? What do you want? What truly matters to you now? Only you can answer those questions.

Creating a new life vision after loss does not mean you are leaving your loved one behind; it means you are daring to imagine a life that continues beyond loss. It reminds you that healing is not just about survival but about rediscovering the possibilities life still holds. Even in the face of deep loss, there is still more to experience, more to give, more to build. The act of envisioning is a radical statement of hope.

Grief shapes us, but it doesn't have to define us. By confronting our pain and envisioning a life larger than our grief, we transform our future and find new meaning in our loss. This transformation honors the love and memories we hold dear while embracing the strength within us to rebuild and grow into a life filled with potential.

What Helped Me: Letter from My Future Self

When developing a vision for the future, sometimes you need a businesslike planning process—that's the type of planning I'm doing as I turn my dream of a nonprofit into reality. But that level of structure can stifle the imagination and might be excessive, depending on where you are in the healing process.

One simple approach I used that helped me think more expansively about the future without overstructuring the process was having my future self write a letter to my current self. If you want to try it, here is the general approach, but customize it to work for you.

Settle yourself in a comfortable space when you have some dedicated time. Center yourself with a grounding exercise, prayer, meditation, or another practice that works for you.

Imagine it is five years (or one year or one month) in the future. You are looking back on your current self and see that you need encouragement, inspiration, and support.

In your journal or on nice stationery, write your current self a letter. Describe your life down the road.

CHAPTER 22: VISION

- What does your day look like?
- How do you feel?
- What have you built?
- What challenges have you faced?
- How did you handle them?
- Who have you built relationships with?
- What impact have you had on your family and community?
- Include anything else you think your current self needs to hear.

Use this letter as your new vision or as the jumping-off place for a more formalized one. As you grow, let your vision grow too. Your evolving vision becomes a testament to your resilience, adaptability, and capacity for hope.

CHAPTER TWENTY-THREE
SELF-TRUST

Dear Drew,
I can still hear your tiny voice calling out,
"Watch me, Mom!" as you jumped down from the tree
you'd climbed with absolutely no fear.
Love, Mom

MY EX-HUSBAND, JOEY, had one pretty great signature move. He would find me on the dance floor and in his goofy-but-charming way say, "Fancy meeting you here. I'm Joey." Then I would laugh and introduce myself too, and for a moment, we would revel in the humor of pretending to flirt with the person we'd been married to for years. It was a simple, silly exchange that somehow always reminded me of the best part of us.

So a few years after we divorced, when I saw Joey on the dance floor at Devin's wedding, I pulled out my best moves, went up to him, and said, "Fancy meeting you here. I'm the mother of the groom." We laughed at our decades-long inside joke and continued to dance with our closest friends and family. Later on, a friend commented on how much fun Joey and I were having. She said she would never be able to dance with her ex-husband, let alone have a meaningful friendship with him. It struck me that our post-divorce relationship might not be all that common.

When Joey and I divorced after twenty-six years, three kids, and multiple affairs, everyone called me crazy for continuing to work with him. But we had spent decades building a family dental practice, and despite the circumstances surrounding our divorce, Joey had asked me to stay with the business. I'd had a tough decision to make.

Even after all his infidelity, I didn't hate Joey. As a husband, he undoubtedly let me down. Joey would probably say that as a wife, I let him down too. Despite my anger, when I filed for divorce, I didn't want to drag him into court. I didn't want to go to war. I wanted to let go of the parts of us that would never work, allow for the parts that could work, and heal what I needed to so that we could both flourish. Trust me, I had a bulldog attorney with plenty of ammunition ready to rip Joey apart, but what outcome would that lead to? If I focused on getting even, there was no way we could continue working together.

I had also seen us go through difficult things in our marriage and still hold our family together. We both had the ability to give our best to our children even if we did not always give our best to each other. Though I couldn't trust Joey with my heart, I knew that if I let the nonfunctional parts of us go, a friendship, business partnership, and co-parenting relationship could still remain—*that* I could trust. Working together would present significant challenges in the short

CHAPTER 23: SELF-TRUST

term, but I knew we could pull it off. I made a clear-eyed choice to continue.

What I did not expect was the pushback I received from everyone else in my life. *No one* supported my idea to stay in business with Joey. They could not understand why I would choose to hold onto any aspect of a relationship that had caused so much hurt. My divorce attorney called it a ridiculously stupid idea and strongly advised against it. Though he ultimately honored my decision, he certainly questioned it the whole way through.

The thing is, while the people in my support system took Joey's offenses personally on my behalf, I already knew Joey's choices had nothing to do with me; they reflected his own challenges and narratives. (See Chapter 16 for more on meaning and interpretation.) If his cheating was not about me, then I didn't need to punish him. Because of my healing work, I had access to a line of thinking based on the relationship I had developed with myself. I could envision potential outcomes that others could not. And I wanted those outcomes more than I wanted to get even. Of course the divorce did not proceed perfectly—divorce is messy and emotional. I struggled. But every time one part of me wanted to let my attorney take over, another part reminded me that our situation was not so black and white.

I chose to think outside the box and trust myself while doing so. And I am thankful I did because it worked. We have scaled the business and are thriving professionally. Joey and I get along better than we ever have, and now I have a different set of tools to use in our interactions. When practiced with intention, they give me a beautiful distance from which to neutrally observe before deciding on a next step that will serve both of us. What everyone else labeled "another one of Melissa's crazy ideas" became the jumping-off point for a lot of healing. Despite our losses and mistakes, our relationship has blossomed into something I truly cherish. I finally have the kind of peaceful relationship I always wanted with Joey, and our family is stronger because of it.

Self-trust strengthens our confidence to make choices that reflect our values and turn our vision into reality.

To create a life bigger than grief, you must not only have a vision, you must trust yourself to bring that vision to fruition. This trust is the foundation upon which resilience is built; it allows you to take risks, embrace uncertainty, and move forward even when the path ahead feels unclear. You are the only one who knows what your life can or should be. You are the only one who can choose your path. While self-trust is needed to make your vision a reality, you might not always feel *confident*, so I want to distinguish the two terms briefly.

Confidence is a feeling of certainty. It reflects a level of comfort that we know what we are doing and what or who we can depend on. Confidence can wax and wane. Especially with new experiences and learning new skills, we may feel a lack of confidence. This is entirely normal. Many people mistakenly believe that confidence must come before action, but in reality, confidence often results from taking action. The more we step forward despite uncertainty, the more confidence we build.

CHAPTER 23: SELF-TRUST

To me, self-trust is deeper than confidence. Self-trust is knowing what we want—our goals and values—and being willing to use our agency to make aligned choices and handle whatever comes as a result. Self-trust does not mean you will never face doubt. Even when you trust yourself, you may feel nervous. Self-trust means you have developed the resilience to move forward despite your doubt. You might not be confident how events will unfold, but you have faith in your skills and capacity to handle whatever happens, to recalibrate and continue. Think of it like driving through fog: You may not see the entire road ahead, but you trust that with each turn of the wheel, more of the path will become visible. The deeper your self-trust becomes, the more confident you are likely to be in your decisions and actions, and you can make decisions that align with your values.

This is the foundation of a life that is truly yours—not shaped by fear, not limited by others' expectations, but guided by the deep knowing within.

However, regardless of whether we have experienced a major loss or trauma, many of us don't trust ourselves. Instead, we look to external sources for validation—our boss, our spouse, the members of our business or social network. In a world that often rewards conformity, it can feel risky to trust our own instincts. The fear of judgment or rejection can paralyze us and lead us to second-guess our choices. We hesitate to launch the business idea we've dreamed of, fearing that others will see us as reckless. We struggle to set firm boundaries, worrying about how they will be received. We replay conversations in our heads, agonizing over whether we said the "right" thing. Each moment of hesitation reinforces the belief that our instincts aren't enough, that we must seek external approval to feel secure. We try to please others, to meet their expectations, to live up to their standards. I am no exception: For much of my life I sought external validation that I was a good wife, a loving mom, and a successful businesswoman.

Without a guarantee that we know exactly how things will turn out and that everyone will approve of us, we feel uncertain. As a result, we end up playing a much smaller game than we are capable of. Or we play someone else's game—not even one that we really want to play. We wait for permission to live fully, when in reality, the only permission we need is our own. We let the fear of looking silly or stupid, the fear of failure, and the fear of what other people think stop us from showing up in the world as our best and highest self.

Now layer in the immense grief that comes with significant loss. After a destabilizing event, confidence and self-trust are shaken. A piece of our identity goes missing, leaving us questioning who we are and where we belong. We doubt our decisions and fear making the wrong choices. You might have spent years being the "go-to" person in your family or workplace, and now, after a major life event, you no longer recognize yourself. It's an identity crisis wrapped in grief, and at times, even the smallest decisions—like what to eat for dinner or what to wear—can overwhelm you. Your internal compass feels shattered; you've been dropped into an unfamiliar city without a map.

But when I lost Drew, I realized that no amount of approval from others could fill the void inside me. I needed to learn how to validate myself. This realization was both liberating and terrifying. It meant that the answers I was searching for weren't out in the world; I had to find them within me.

Recovering self-trust—or building it for the first time—is challenging. The good news is that self-trust is a skill, a muscle that can be strengthened, and as you do the hard work of healing, you are

CHAPTER 23: SELF-TRUST

surely developing it. How can you survive loss, develop new tools, and face the tough stuff and *not* develop self-trust? As you heal, you learn to listen, to connect to your heart, and to lead from a place of love and compassion. You start to recognize where you have room to grow, and you begin showing yourself the support you need to prioritize that growth. By creating a loving relationship with yourself, you learn to show yourself grace while processing whatever challenges you face. This relationship with yourself keeps you steady when the world around you feels uncertain. You learn to trust yourself to navigate life with agency and authenticity. You stand firm in your decisions even when those around you do not understand or agree. Self-trust means you listen to your own inner voice and choose alignment over approval.

All the tools and skills we've talked about in this book support you in building self-trust, but more specific to this topic, here are a few practical tactics.

Recognize your patterns. We all have different areas where we trust ourselves and where we want external validation. When making a decision, ask yourself:

- Am I making this choice for myself, or to please someone else?
- What do I want in this situation?
- How can I honor my needs without seeking permission from others?

Each time you pause to ask these questions, you create space between impulse and action. That space allows you to choose from a place of alignment rather than fear.

Simply noticing when you seek external validation can help refocus and modify behavior. If you are nervous about making a particular choice, look at some of your past decisions that turned out well. Maybe you once doubted your ability to move to a new city alone, yet you made it work. Maybe you feared leaving a job but in hindsight found it the best decision you ever made. Finding tangible proof of your capability rewires the brain to trust itself. Look for evidence that reinforces the belief that you are capable. (Revisit Chapter 15 for a refresher on shaping narratives.) The more you lean into self-trust, the less external validation you need.

Focus on consistency. Think about what makes you trust someone else: Their words align with their actions. They follow through on their promises. Over time, their consistency builds trust. The same principle applies: Self-trust and confidence grow when we make and keep promises to ourselves. Make yourself a promise that you will keep for thirty days. (You might choose an area in which you have noticed a pattern of seeking external approval.) Consistency in fulfilling the promise is more important than the promise itself, so start small if you need to and build from there. For example, commit to drinking a glass of water first thing in the morning or to journaling for five minutes each night. These seemingly minor acts become proof that you can rely on yourself. Every time you follow through, you fortify your inner trust, building it into confidence that doesn't depend on anyone else. Those small steps lead to big change. Over time, you recognize that you are capable and worthy of more than you thought possible, and the momentum becomes difficult to derail.

Clarify your values. If you are regularly pausing to ask yourself what you want and the answer is unclear, it might be time to step back and reassess your values. Your values act as an internal compass, guiding you toward choices that feel right, even when the path is uncertain. Decisions feel easier when they align with what matters most. It's not that you don't have values—of course you have values!—but you might not have articulated them clearly. A lack of clarity can come into play on decisions in which two or more values are competing and, of course, when your personal values conflict with societal norms. For example, you may deeply value stability, but you also crave adventure. If you aren't aware of this internal tension, you might struggle with decisions like changing careers or moving to a new city. You might feel stuck in a job you dislike because stability was once your top value but now freedom or passion has risen in importance.

For a quick assessment, print out a list of personal values (search "values list" online), and circle the five to seven that are most important to you. The next time you face a decision, consult that list. Instead of asking what you should do, try asking: Which choice aligns with my highest values?

Find a coach or mentor. When you are developing the self-trust and confidence to bring your vision to life, coaches and mentors can be beneficial. I will note here that therapists and counselors, who may help you in the early stages of grief (and for many other reasons), usually focus on processing past events and related emotions. Coaches and mentors typically focus on the future and helping you make the changes—mindset, behavioral, and so on—needed to achieve your goals. Both types of assistance are valuable. Here, I am talking about future-focused assistance.

Mentors are especially helpful when you are looking for guidance from someone who has trodden a similar path. When I began public speaking, for instance, I had other speakers who mentored me as to how the speaking industry worked. They gave me practical advice on how to develop new engagements, shared tips for engaging an audience, and answered the numerous questions I had. This was when I truly learned the value of the old adage "the only stupid question is the unasked one." My mentors helped me see possibilities that I couldn't yet see for myself; they expanded my vision of what was possible.

Coaches tend to give less advice and instead help you find your own answers. They act as sounding boards, whether about your vision and goals or about challenges you face. They also act as mirrors, reflecting things you can't necessarily see about yourself. This kind of reflection can be uncomfortable, but it is also an opportunity for profound growth. The best coaches don't just tell you what you want to hear; they challenge you to step into your fullest potential and help you stay accountable to your stated values and goals. I'll never forget Rev. Kev gently calling me out for being late to our meeting and not having my homework completely done: "I need you to try a new way of being. Treat this as sacred space. Be in integrity." That moment was a turning point for me in realizing that self-trust isn't just about belief—it's about action.

Adjust your success/failure mindset. One of the big, big snares we catch ourselves in is the fear of failure. Sometimes things don't go as planned, but that doesn't make the effort a "failure." (And "failure" by whose definition?) I have adopted the mindset that even a "failure" is not a failure—it is merely a lesson. Reframing failure as feedback allows you to take risks without the paralyzing fear of making mistakes.

Can I tell you how many times things haven't gone to plan for me? One time, I launched a webinar series, and a single person showed up. As a result, I realized my marketing wasn't reaching the people I wanted; I had allowed the PR folks to sway me in a direction that was ineffective. I could have labeled the whole experience a failure, but instead, I chose to see it as valuable market research, and what I learned ultimately led to a much more successful strategy. I want to point out that it takes practice to discern when to lean on experts and when to trust your gut; after all, experts are experts for a reason. Just remember that nothing is wasted. Look for the gems—what you can learn and how you can grow.

Learn to recalibrate and let go. When things don't work as planned, sometimes the change needed is obvious and you can try again. Sometimes you don't know what to change; you might have to recalibrate and try an entirely different approach. Trusting yourself means trusting your ability to adapt, even when the path forward is unclear. Getting to your goal or vision is not a straight journey; you will zigzag. Stay focused on the vision, and try anything you need to that is aligned to it. When you have set aside the black-and-white success/failure mindset, attempting new things is much more fun! It's like trying on jeans: many pairs won't fit, but one will, and it will look great.

Recalibration doesn't mean you've failed; it just means you are evolving.

One of the hardest things about recalibration is that it sometimes means you have to let something go, whether people, mentors, processes, or your own expectations. Things that might have worked in the past no longer do. You can follow a mentor's path for a while, but eventually you must break new ground. As you grow and as your vision grows, you will likely need new approaches, and you might need different team members to support you.

Remember playing on the monkey bars as a kid? You essentially hang from a horizontal ladder and try to make your way across rung by rung, but you can't move to the next rung unless you let go of the current one. Each transition in life requires a moment of trust, a moment where you must release the old before fully grasping the new. You might not feel confident, but you have to trust the rung will be there when your hand reaches forward. And occasionally, you fall in the sand. Falling isn't failure. It's part of learning how to swing forward. Each time you make it another rung though, you learn what you are capable of. Yes, letting go can be hard. But it's necessary for growth. This is the gift of choice and agency. We get to grow and develop. We can't go back, but we can take the most important elements forward.

• • •

Having a strong relationship with yourself allows you the confidence to trust your decisions, let go of external validation, and move forward with clarity and purpose. As self-trust grows, confidence grows, and it eventually transforms into courage to dream bigger, take risks, and build a life aligned with who you authentically are. The journey from self-trust to courage isn't always linear, but each step forward reinforces the belief that you are capable, resilient, and worthy of living fully. And when you trust yourself deeply enough, you realize that no matter what happens, you will find a way forward.

What Helped Me: Seeking Discomfort

Part of learning to trust yourself is learning that you can come through discomfort just fine, and in fact may benefit from it. Discomfort expands your "game board." One of the things that helped me was seeking out situations that made me uncomfortable, stretching myself out of my comfort zone. But I started small, with low-stakes experiments and actions. I found that as my game board expanded, I played a bigger game.

If you want to try this, here are some ideas to get you started.

Choose a new skill to learn. Making mistakes is part of the learning process. Pick something to learn at which you are a beginner. If you would like to learn to be a better public speaker (most people's number one fear), visit a Toastmasters club. If you want to learn the technique of watercolor painting, take an adult ed class. Get comfortable having things turn out not quite as you envisioned them.

Ask an uncomfortable question. The fear of appearing "stupid" often holds us back from asking questions. Don't let it. If you didn't follow a conversation at work, ask a colleague to get you up to speed. If you don't understand the stock market and the best way to invest your 401(k) money, ask your financial planner for guidance. Notice how you feel after getting an answer.

Ask for feedback. Listening to what others think of you or your work can feel vulnerable. Ask someone you trust for feedback on a piece of writing or a presentation you gave at work. Ask for one thing you did well and one thing that would enhance your effectiveness at that task. With practice, you will hone your ability to discern when to incorporate feedback and when not to.

Set a boundary. Those of us who like to please other people often struggle to set boundaries for fear of causing disappointment. Set a reasonable boundary that is in your own best interest: decide you will be done working at 5 p.m. daily or that you will always take Sunday as a "day of rest" and not answer work emails.

After you stretch into the zone of discomfort, reflect on how the experience felt. How will it feel the next time you do it? What benefit did you find in getting outside your comfort zone? How will this support you as you turn your vision into a reality?

CHAPTER TWENTY-FOUR

LOVE

Dear Drew,
Thank you for being my guiding light
on this journey of healing.
Love, Mom

WHEN I FIRST MET GRIEF, I was ten years old and navigating the impending loss of my mother to cancer. I didn't have the emotional tools or maturity to comprehend the vastness of death or the fullness of life in its presence. Instead, I had a solitary, threatening narrative: Grief was a dark, looming consequence destined to destroy our lives. *Someday she is going to die,* I thought, *so don't upset her. Don't be too loud. Don't make a mess.* Grief taught me avoidance. Our family didn't dare talk about death. Instead, we clung to gratitude with a white-knuckled grip: *She is alive; be grateful.* I did the best I could with this limited perspective, striving to be the good child, the good sister, the good student. For a time, this shield of perfection protected me from the chaos within my family. But it also taught me to suppress my grief—to hide it away like an unwelcome guest.

In my teenage years, as friendships fractured and romantic relationships dissolved, I leaned on this same flawed understanding of grief. When relationships in my early adult years failed to provide the love and safety I yearned for, I came to a simple but devastating conclusion: I must not have been good enough. This belief, forged in childhood, became the lens through which I saw myself. It turned me into an apprehensive, self-doubting young wife and mother who looked to everyone but herself for validation, support, and happiness.

Then came Drew.

Drew's passing shattered the inadequate framework of grief I had constructed over the years. Continuing to believe the damning narratives I was telling myself would have killed me. I had to make a different choice. I could no longer live with that version of grief. I had to find a way to transform the suffocating pain into something resembling peace, something life-giving and meaningful. It seemed impossible, a fool's errand.

I could have swallowed those pills. I could have drowned myself in alcohol, shopping, or other artificial forms of relief. I could have stomped around my emotional swampland forever, reveling in the splatter of the sludge. But instead, I chose to mine the gems buried in the mud of my pain. I decided to unearth every ribbon of value and extract every carat of wisdom I could. It was exhausting, heartbreaking work—work I never asked for—but those beautiful gems, pried loose from the depths of my heart and soul, returned their investment a thousand times over.

By consciously choosing healing, I reimagined what Drew's loss could mean. Following my intuition, I began to transform both my greatest gifts and my most devastating experiences into a force for good. I didn't want the pain of my loss to diminish my contribution to the world. Instead, I allowed it to guide me toward my truest path and purpose. I cherish the changes I've undergone as Drew's mother. His life and loss have shaped me into someone who deeply values empathy, compassion, resilience, and the preciousness of life.

At the heart of my healing lies one undeniable truth: love.

WE ARE FOREVER CHANGED BY LOSS; LOVE LETS US CHOOSE HOW.

Love gives us the strength to reimagine grief, to see beyond its pain and into its potential. Love transforms the darkest moments into a path of light and growth. Love is the constant force that tethers us to humanity and guides us toward hope. Love is more than a feeling. It is a practice, a tool, and a force we can harness to navigate grief. When we embrace love as a healing strategy, we unlock its potential to restore us, to teach us, and to help us rebuild.

For me, love became my most powerful ally in three profound ways.

First, my love for Drew never diminished. Despite his physical absence, my love for him deepened and expanded, becoming a force that drove me to celebrate his memory. Every act of healing, every choice to rise above the pain, became a tribute to the love we shared. By focusing on that love, I created a bridge between my grief and my hope.

Second, healing required learning to love myself—not in spite of my grief but because of it. Embracing the parts of myself that felt broken, scared, and inadequate was the hardest but most transformative step. Love taught me to see my pain as part of my humanity and my resilience as a testament to my strength.

Third, grief opened my heart to the struggles of those around me, teaching me to love more deeply and broadly and to extend compassion and understanding to those navigating their own losses. Through this outward expression of love, I found connection and purpose.

Ultimately, my journey through grief taught me that love never dies; it simply transforms. I still have a relationship with Drew. It looks different now, but it is no less real to me than the days I gave him rocky road ice cream for breakfast and watched him run through cornfields in the evening light.

Some people say that grief is love with nowhere to go. I think grief is love that still exists—loud, present, and searching for the place it knows by heart. It is not a void. It is not an ending. It is love expanding, stretching beyond what our human senses can grasp.

What we feel in grief is not the absence of love but the ache of its continued presence. Love doesn't disappear when a life ends; it shifts. It moves from something we hold in our hands to something we carry in our being. Grief is the longing to touch that love again— to feel it, to know it, to remember that it never left.

This isn't about denying the pain. Grief hurts because love matters. But pain isn't the whole story. Grief can also be the doorway to a deeper truth that love is not bound by time, form, or death. Love is energy. It's eternal. It moves with us, through us, and far beyond us. When we open ourselves to that reality, we stop seeing grief as an endpoint. We start seeing it as a passageway—love's way of reaching back toward connection. The pain we feel is love trying to say, "I'm still here."

No one escapes life untouched by loss—the death of loved ones, the loss of jobs, the end of relationships. We often do everything we can to avoid it, but if we embrace grief as more than sadness and pain, it offers astonishing gifts. Reimagined through the lens of love,

CHAPTER 24: LOVE

grief becomes a teacher that reveals the multifaceted nature of our humanity and leads us on a profound journey of transformation. By choosing to ask grief what it can teach us, we uncover lessons about ourselves, the world, and who we want to be within it.

Grief doesn't shrink with time; instead, we must use love to grow larger than grief. By building a life expansive enough to hold both grief and joy, we create space for healing and maturing. Each step along the healing path strengthens our inner and outer worlds. And while grief might feel destructive, it is also generative. It is meant to change us, to bring us closer to our truest identity. When we trust grief enough to let it transform us, it invites us to meet our most enlightened self. But first, we must welcome it.

Healing is not an accident; it is an intentional, ongoing choice. Over twenty years ago, I chose to heal both for myself and for Drew. I chose to reimagine his loss as a source of wisdom, to transform his absence into a presence that guides and uplifts me. Today, I know with certainty that healing is possible and that love transcends physical existence. Grief does not define us; our choices in its presence do. By meeting grief with courage, resilience, grace, and yes, love, we emerge stronger, more compassionate, and more capable of creating a life filled with joy and purpose. We are forever changed by loss, but love lets us choose how.

So when grief comes, wrap your arms around it and say, "Teach me. Guide me. I am ready." Let it shape you into the person you were meant to be. Let love be your compass, your teacher, your strength. Embrace grief not as an end but as a catalyst for your most beautiful and meaningful evolution.

What Helped Me: The Love Lens

To integrate love into your healing journey, I encourage you to adopt what I call the "love lens." This simple but profound mindset helped me approach grief with love as my guiding principle. Here are different ways to use it:

Pause and reflect. When grief feels overwhelming, take a moment to reflect on the love embedded within your loss. Who or what did you love that caused this pain? Let that love remind you of the connection and meaning that still exist.

Reframe the pain. Instead of focusing solely on what you've lost, ask yourself: What does this loss reveal about the depth of my love? How can I carry that love forward? Use these questions to shift your perspective from loss to gratitude.

Act with love. Take one small action each day that bears witness to the love you feel. You could write a letter to your loved one, practice self-care, or extend kindness to someone else. Let love guide your actions.

Invite love to teach you. Sit with your grief and ask yourself: What does love want me to learn from this experience? Trust that love will reveal lessons about resilience, compassion, and purpose.

You carry within you the agency to choose, the resilience to grow, and the capacity to heal. Trust that love will guide you forward.

CONCLUSION

IF YOU ARE HERE, in the final pages of this book, then you have already begun your journey. You have wrestled with your grief, explored the possibilities beyond it, and, I hope, discovered a glimpse of what is waiting for you on the other side. I want to leave you with one final truth: Life beyond grief is not only possible—it is yours to claim.

Grief has a way of making us feel small, limited, and trapped within a single identity: someone who has experienced loss. But you are more than your loss. The work I have done, the work I have asked you to do throughout this book, is what allowed me to see that. It is what untethered me from a life that was about only my grief and opened me to something bigger.

At the start of my journey, I longed to understand how to live in a world that had taken so much from me. But through the process of exploration, realignment, and deep self-work, I have come to yearn for something more: expansion. The loss I once feared would define me has instead shaped me into someone who can hold sorrow and joy, grief and gratitude, pain and possibility—all at once.

The healing journey is deeply personal, and the outcome will look different for everyone. But the potential is the same: a life that is fuller, richer, and more meaningful because of what you have endured. Grief strips away the unnecessary. It forces you to see what truly matters. And once you have seen it, you can never go back to who you were before. That is the gift hidden within the pain.

I still mourn my son, and I will always miss him. But I also still know him; I still feel him. And because of that, his loss was not just an ending; it became the reason I found a new beginning. It is why I discovered hope again. It is why I know, without a doubt, that even when life takes an unexpected turn, joy is still possible. It may require searching and work, but it is always there, waiting to be found.

This is what I want for you. Not just healing, but wholeness. Not just survival, but expansion. You have done the hard work of facing your grief, examining your pain, and allowing yourself to imagine something beyond it. That is no small feat. It is a testament to your strength, resilience, and faith.

You will still have moments when grief feels overwhelming. That is normal. Healing is not linear, and expansion does not mean the absence of sorrow. But now you have tools to navigate those moments differently. You know that pain does not have to consume you. You know that grief does not have to be the final word. You know that within you lies the power to create a life that is not defined by what you have lost but by what you still have and what you can become.

If you take nothing else from this book, I hope you take this: You are allowed to dream again. You are allowed to love again. You are allowed to feel joy without guilt, to hold hope without hesitation, and to live fully without apology. Carry your memories, your lessons, your pain, and your love with you. Let them guide you, but do not let them limit you.

You may not have all the answers yet, but life is not about having all the answers. It is about being willing to ask the questions, staying open to possibility, and trusting that the road ahead, no matter how uncertain, holds something worth walking toward. So step forward with courage. Step forward with hope. And when doubt creeps in, remind yourself of the work you have done, the truths you have uncovered, and the strength you have found within yourself.

The journey continues, and I am cheering you on.

AFTERWORD

August 14, 2024

DEAR DREW,

Tomorrow marks your twenty-ninth birthday, a poignant reminder that I was twenty-nine when you left us. As I sit here reflecting on the years that have passed, I am struck by the depth of my grief and by the strength I have found within myself.

Losing you was the most profound pain I have ever known. The days, months, and years that followed were filled with an aching void, a constant reminder of your absence. I grieved deeply, Drew, in ways that words can scarcely capture. My sorrow was a heavy, all-consuming weight that felt impossible to bear. And yet, amid the darkness of my grief, I discovered a resilience I never knew I possessed.

Your memory has become a beacon of love, guiding me through the storms and challenges of life. Somehow I've learned to navigate the waves of grief, to find moments of peace and even joy. I've grown in ways I never imagined possible.

I often wonder what you would be like today, at twenty-nine. Would you have your brother's sense of humor? His gentle spirit? Or your sister's kind heart and quick wit? Would you share my passion for helping others, for finding meaning in the midst of chaos? These questions linger in my heart, unanswered, yet they bring a sense of closeness to you, as if you are still here guiding me.

Your life, though tragically short, has left an indelible mark on my soul. I have dedicated myself to helping others who walk this path of loss, finding purpose in the pain. Through my work, I hope to honor your memory, ensuring that your spirit continues to touch the lives of others.

Today, I am reminded that even in the face of unimaginable loss, there is a way to move forward. It is not about forgetting or moving on but about carrying the love and memories with us, allowing them to shape us into stronger, more compassionate beings.

As I write this, I feel your presence, a comforting reminder that you are never truly gone. You live on in my heart, in the memories we share at family gatherings, in the work I do, and in the lives of those you have touched through me.

Your spirit is a constant source of inspiration, a reminder of the beauty and fragility of life. I honor the love we shared, the lessons you have taught me, and the strength I have found in your absence. You are my guiding light, my eternal source of love and resilience.

Happy birthday, my precious son. I celebrate all the good your life has brought us. You are forever loved, forever missed, and forever remembered.

With all my love,
Mom

ACKNOWLEDGMENTS

THIS BOOK REPRESENTS a deeply personal journey of healing, growth, and resilience. I could not have arrived at this moment without the unwavering support, encouragement, and guidance of many remarkable individuals.

To Laurie Campbell: Your steadfast belief in my vision and your invaluable connection to Lisa Hagan, my incredible literary agent, have been pivotal in bringing this dream to life. Your faith in me has been a source of light during some of my darkest times.

To Kirsten Quinn, who helped me begin writing my manuscript, and Karin Wiberg, who helped me carry it across the finish line: Your dedication to editing and refining my manuscript has been nothing short of extraordinary. Your insights, attention to detail, and creative input have given shape and clarity to my words, and for that, I am forever grateful.

To Health Communications, Inc., and Christine Belleris: Thank you for seeing the potential in my story and granting me the opportunity to share it with the world. Your belief in this project has meant everything.

To the Reverend Kevin Kitrell Ross, Sylvia High, Tam Pendleton, and Robin Johnson: Each of you has played a vital role in my healing journey. Your wisdom, encouragement, and kindness have inspired me to embrace my story and share it with others.

To Dr. Larry Drell: Your compassionate guidance through some of my most difficult moments gave me the tools to face my pain and begin to heal. Your support has been a true gift.

To Star Rose Bond: Your raw and honest mentorship challenged me to dream bigger and see the beauty in life again. You have been an anchor in my transformation, and I am deeply grateful.

To my incredible team: Jose Castro, thank you for keeping everything running smoothly at the dental practices; your hard work and dedication allow me to focus on my greater mission. Farras Seay, I am beyond grateful for your organization and support seamlessly filling in the gaps while I poured myself into completing *Dear Drew*; I couldn't have done this without you.

To Jane and Porfirio: The fun we share on and off the tennis court has been a true gift. You have no idea how much your friendship means to me—your laughter, camaraderie, and unwavering support have brightened so many moments.

To my dear friends: Your encouragement, love, and support over the years have meant more to me than words can express. Your presence in my life has been a source of strength, and I am endlessly grateful for each of you.

To my cherished family, especially my sister Jennifer and my Aunt Debbie: Your love, support, and unwavering presence have been a foundation of strength for me. Thank you for standing by me through everything—for lifting me up, believing in me, and reminding me that I am never alone. I also want to honor my beloved mother and grandmother, whose lives were powerful examples of resilience and strength. They showed me how to stand tall through adversity and love without condition. Their unwavering support and boundless love shaped who I am, and I carry them with me always.

To Theresa: Though we have never met, your letter was a lifeline in my time of unimaginable pain. Your words gave me hope when I felt hopeless, and for that, I owe you more than I can ever express.

Finally, to my readers: Thank you for opening your hearts to my story. It is my hope that this book offers you comfort, connection, and courage on your own healing journey.

RESOURCES

Tools on My Website

In each chapter I have provided What Helped Me tools to aid in the healing process. On my website, you can find expanded versions of the exercises, additional examples, free downloads, and more.

Just go to melissahull.com and look for "Dear Drew Extended Resources."

Books

I have found books enormously helpful in the healing process, as they offer insight, consolation, and encouragement. Here are some of my favorites.

Cameron, Julia. 1992. *The Artist's Way: A Spiritual Path to Higher Creativity.* New York: TarcherPerigee. A twelve-week program intended to increase creativity by capturing the creative energy of the universe.

Chamine, Shirzad. 2012. *Positive Intelligence: Why Only 20% of Teams and Individuals Achieve Their True Potential and How You Can Achieve Yours.* Austin, TX: Greenleaf Book Group Press. Discusses mental fitness and strategies for achieving peak performance and happiness.

Eden, Donna, and David Feinstein. 1998. *Energy Medicine: Balance Your Body's Energies for Optimum Health, Joy, and Vitality.* New York: Tarcher. Details methods for balancing and enhancing body energy for health and vitality.

Eden, Donna, and David Feinstein. 2008. *Energy Medicine for Women: Aligning Your Body's Energies to Boost Your Health and Vitality.* New York: TarcherPerigee. Details methods for balancing and enhancing body energy for health and vitality.

Foundation for Inner Peace. 1975. *A Course in Miracles: Workbook for Students.* Novato, CA: Foundation for Inner Peace. Serves as a spiritual guide for inner peace and self-awareness.

Hawkins, David R. 2020. *The Map of Consciousness Explained: A Proven Energy Scale to Actualize Your Ultimate Potential.* Carlsbad, CA: Hay House. Explores the energy of emotions and how to shift their frequency.

High, Sylvia. 2015. *The Little Book of Big Questions: A Journey in Self Discovery.* Self-published. Encourages deep introspection through thought-provoking questions.

Johnson, Robin. 2021. *Heart-Centered Life Coaching Training Manual.* Farmington, UT: The Heart Coach Institute. Provides a comprehensive guide combining the power of life coaching with the wisdom of the heart.

McNeal, Delatorro L., II. 2013. *Thriving Through Your Storms: 12 Profound Lessons to Help You Grow Through Anything You Go Through in Life.* Platinum Performance Global. Outlines lessons for resilience and growth through challenging times.

Nelson, Bradley. 2023. *The Body Code: Unlocking Your Body's Ability to Heal Itself.* New York: St. Martin's Essentials. Introduces techniques to unlock natural healing potential.

Pendleton, Tam. 2018. *The Healer's Blueprint,* 4th ed. Freedom Body Works. Provides a comprehensive guide for energy healing practices.

Ponder, Catherine. 1966. *The Dynamic Laws of Healing.* Camarillo, CA: DeVorss Publications. Focuses on spiritual and financial abundance.

Ponder, Catherine. 1971. *Open Your Mind to Prosperity.* Camarillo, CA: DeVorss Publications. Focuses on spiritual and financial abundance.

Ponder, Catherine. 1981. *The Secret of Unlimited Prosperity.* Camarillo, CA: DeVorss Publications. Focuses on spiritual and financial abundance.

Ross, Kevin Kitrell. 2012. *The Designer Life: Distinctions for Living Life by Design and Not by Default,* 2nd ed. Self-published. Provides practical distinctions for living intentionally and designing life instead of living by default.

Ross, Kevin Kitrell, and Eric Ovid Donaldson. 2021. *Breathing Space: A 52-Week Meditation Journey for Centered, Soulful, and Successful Living.* Self-published. Offers weekly meditations to foster a centered, soulful, and successful lifestyle.

Sadler, Staci. 2013. *Aura Personalities: Our Innate Gifts and Magnified Potential Reflected in the Energy We Emanate.* Orem, UT: McNeil Printing. Explores the interplay of energy and innate gifts.

Unity Church. n.d. *Strength, Courage, and Comfort for Difficult Times.* Unity Village, MO: Unity Church. Delivers spiritual insights for overcoming life's challenges.

Willis, Marilyn. 2020. *Restored: A Self-Paced Grief Workbook for Your Journey from Loss to Life.* Valley, CA: Zamiz Press. Designed to help navigate the journey from loss to life.

Healing Modalities

Throughout this book I mention various healing modalities I have tried over the past few decades. Here is a complete list. You may wish to explore any that resonate.

Mind-Body Practices

- Meditation: Mindfulness and relaxation practices
- Yoga: Physical postures combined with breathwork and meditation
- Tai Chi / Qigong: Gentle physical exercises with a focus on energy flow
- Hypnotherapy: Guided hypnosis for psychological healing
- Visualization / Guided Imagery: Technique using mental imagery for healing and stress reduction

Energy-Based Therapies

- Reiki: Japanese energy healing technique
- Healing Touch: Energy therapy involving gentle touch or close placement of the hands near the receiver's body
- Chakra Balancing: Restoring balance to energy centers
- Acupuncture: Inserting thin needles into the skin along the energy meridians
- Craniosacral Therapy: Gentle manipulation of the skull and spine
- Sound Healing: Using sound frequencies (e.g., tuning forks, singing bowls)
- Cellular Energy Release: Therapeutic technique that focuses on releasing deeply stored emotional and physical trauma at a cellular level

- Sacred Heart Therapy: A meditative and spiritual practice that focuses on connecting with the heart's energy to cultivate inner peace, healing, and a deeper sense of connections to oneself and the divine

Natural and Traditional Medicine

- Herbal Medicine: Using plant-based remedies
- Ayurveda: Traditional Indian system of medicine
- Naturopathy: Healing through diet, exercise, and natural remedies
- Aromatherapy: Using essential oils for therapeutic effects

Manual and Physical Therapies

- Massage Therapy: Manipulation of muscles and soft tissues
- Chiropractic Care: Adjustments to the spine and joints
- Acupressure: Applying pressure to points on the feet, hands, or ears
- Breath Work: Practice the conscious control of the breath to improve mental, emotional, and physical well-being
- Somatic Therapy: Body-centric psychotherapy

Creative Arts Therapies

- Art Therapy: Using art for emotional expression and healing
- Music Therapy: Healing through music creation and listening

- Dance/Movement Therapy: Using movement for emotional and physical healing
- Drama Therapy: Role-play and storytelling for therapeutic purposes

Spiritual and Indigenous Practices

- Shamanic Healing: Traditional practices by Indigenous healers, or practices with origins in Indigenous cultures
- Prayer and Faith Healing: Spiritual interventions for healing
- Soul Retrieval: Reintegrating fragmented parts of the soul
- Channeling: Guidance, healing, or messages from spiritual sources, often with the facilitation of medium, psychic, or other spirit worker

ABOUT THE AUTHOR

MELISSA HULL is an internationally recognized voice in grief recovery, particularly for parents healing from child loss. A certified master coach, award-winning artist, and healthcare CEO, she has changed countless lives through her powerful message of resilience and transformation. Her work has been featured on has changed countless lives MSNBC and Fox, and in *Forbes, Glamour,* and *USA Today*. She is also the recipient of multiple presidential awards and an honorary doctorate of humanitarianism.